JAMES COLLINS

ELECTRIC GUITARS

a practical guide to set up,
maintenance and repair

JAMES COLLINS

ELECTRIC GUITARS

a practical guide to set up,
maintenance and repair

THE CROWOOD PRESS

Contents

Introduction 6

PART 1: **GUITAR SETUP** 9

CHAPTER 1: **Assessment and Understanding the Numbers** 11
CHAPTER 2: **Neck Relief and How to Adjust** 17
CHAPTER 3: **String Height Action** 29
CHAPTER 4: **Bridge Saddle Radius** 37
CHAPTER 5: **Floating the Bridge** 43
CHAPTER 6: **Intonation** 49

PART 2: **GUITAR MAINTENANCE** 55

CHAPTER 7: **Fretboards** 57
CHAPTER 8: **Fret Polishing** 61
CHAPTER 9: **Electrics** 65
CHAPTER 10: **General Cleaning** 69
CHAPTER 11: **Re-Stringing** 73
CHAPTER 12: **Pickup Heights** 93
Full Setup, Start to Finish: Gibson Les Paul Standard 96
Full Setup, Start to Finish: Fender Stratocaster 103

PART 3: **GUITAR REPAIR** 109

CHAPTER 13: **Basics** 110
CHAPTER 14: **Nuts** 115
CHAPTER 15: **Machine Heads** 126
CHAPTER 16: **Electrics** 130
CHAPTER 17: **Fret Dressing** 136
CHAPTER 18: **Re-Fretting** 149
CHAPTER 19: **Broken Headstocks** 158
CHAPTER 20: **Finishing** 167

Index 173

Introduction

My background

The early days of my lutherie journey began with me basically taking apart all my guitars, 'cleaning' them and then trying to put them back together. It was a great initial learning experience. After suffering a headstock break on my first Les Paul and having it 'repaired' badly three times – it would keep opening up again, because the wrong glue had been used – a good friend suggested that I should go and study guitar repair and fix the break myself. (I have now carried out that particular repair hundreds of times without it reopening.) I had worked in the music industry for many years after leaving college, but somewhere along the way I had fallen out of love with it. After consulting with a few knowledgeable friends, I decided to head out to Michigan to attend the Galloup School of Lutherie, run by Bryan Galloup. The school already had a very good reputation, but it was not quite as big as it is now. I found myself in a small class with six other students, all eager to learn guitar building and repair. From the very early days, we were taught

the philosophy that a good guitar builder is a great repairer.

Having completed my studies in 2007, I returned to the UK. I had been impressed with the professionalism that had been taught at Galloup and I wanted to emulate this approach, and establish a guitar service and repair centre of the type that seemed to me to be lacking in the UK. At that time, most setup work, for example, was done in the back room of the shop that sold the guitars. My company 12th Fret Guitar Setup and Repair came into being at the start of 2008 and I certainly hit the ground running! Looking back, I feel now that the first couple of years of 12th Fret were my real apprenticeship. It was a steep learning curve, but I had been well schooled in the fundamentals at Galloup. Within two years 12th Fret became one of four Gibson service centres, undertaking Gibson warranty work. The association helped the business to expand and during those first three years the repair benches and racks were always full.

After a while I was asked by a guitar school to share my knowledge about guitar setup and maintenance by giving

Setup tools.

some lectures to their students. They had realised that of the few hundred students of all ages who attended the school, hardly any knew how to look after their instruments properly. Only a handful knew how to change strings, let alone anything else. Generally, they were leaving it to the local shop to do, which was fine, but it did not happen regularly enough. As a result, many of the students were not playing the guitar as often as they should or, sadly, were not enjoying it when they did. Dirty old strings do not feel great under the hand and do not intonate as well as newer, cleaner ones. The inevitable knock-on effect is that the guitar does not get played as much.

After that first day of three lectures to groups of 20, when I showed them how to re-string and clean up their fretboards, clean out the pots, and so on, the feedback from the school was very positive. Many more students were playing the guitar more often, and fulfilling the requirements of their study, after finally changing their strings. A welcome side effect was the number who came to visit the workshop, to ask me to do a complete setup on their guitar. My work at the guitar school was not only enjoyable and satisfying, it was also good for business!

That first foray into teaching led to the establishment of guitar tech courses based on the same philosophy as those at the Galloup School: if you can build it, you can repair it. The three-day build course covered many tech skills as well as everything to do with getting the guitar set up well. Initially, attendees would learn how to assemble a Strat from quality parts, but more recently I have offered courses on building a Stratocaster, Telecaster or Jazzmaster, explaining in the process how to fit machine heads, how to understand scale length and bridge positioning, the fitting and soldering of all the electrics, fret dressing, making a bone nut and how to get the setup right. The result at the end of the course is a terrific guitar! There are many independent repairs and modifications within the build, all of which are covered in the book. Many techs have taken part, as well as students of all ages, learning how to assemble their guitars and understanding each part of the build as a repair. Teaching all aspects of the course has really helped cement my own understanding and passion for all the processes that make up guitar setup, maintenance and repair.

After the first year of guitar-building courses, I introduced a Pro Guitar Setup course, which teaches guitar setup through theory and practice over one day. After more than a decade, this is still very well attended by all levels and ages of guitarist, as well as some great roadies/techs seeking to broaden or freshen up their skills. The other students always enjoy having a touring tech alongside them, especially when they share their insights and stories of touring musicians during lunch! It is a great day of delving into how to get the best out of both your own guitar and the guitars of others. This is what I hope this book will bring to you.

The business now also incorporates the hand-building of boutique electric guitars under my own name, putting all my years of setup and repair into making the best guitars I can. My experience with setting up and repair, and with delivering the building courses, has led me to discover and use hardware materials and electrical components of the best quality. I am a frequent visitor to the excellent specialist wood yard that is close to my workshops, and I take real pleasure in working with their woods to create guitars for customers old and new.

Overview of the book

The purpose of the book is to show you how to get the best out of your own guitars and those of others. It will look closely at all aspects of electric guitar setup, the setup points for all four- and five-string basses and six-string electrics, as well as twelve-string, multiple-scale lengths too. The whole process and application will be explained, for beginners, intermediate and professional techs. Having taught guitar setup in the UK for many years, I have come to the conclusion that the one aspect missing most from people's knowledge is the ability to assess the guitar's current setup in the correct order. Chapter 1 will cover in detail the order of assessment and explain how to understand the numbers.

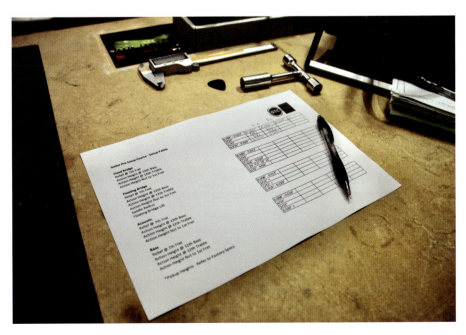

Mapping out the setup points.

James Collins guitar showroom.

Learning how to get the best out of the setup on your guitar will really help with your playing and learning, and encourage your passion for the guitar. In assessing your own guitar, a consideration of your playing style is important if you are to get the best out of it. You may be lucky enough to have a few guitars that can be set up for different genres – or you may decide to buy some more! It is possible, however, to get the setup right so that it suits a range of genres.

When setting up a guitar for someone else, your aim should be to understand and translate what they want from the guitar and its setup. This requires a good understanding of where the current numbers are on the guitar and an ability to interpret that in order to achieve the optimum setup for both guitar and player. Good assessment is always key.

With each part to the setup points laid out in the following chapters, the theory will show you the reasons *why* you should adopt a particular approach, rather than just telling you *how* to do the setup work. I have felt through teaching that people have often been told how to do something without a proper explanation. Simply copying a process without having any deeper understanding can be confusing, especially in the area of neck relief adjustment. The theory is important, and practice and experience certainly account for a lot, but a deeper understanding will complete the picture.

As well as guitar setup and maintenance, the book will also cover many aspects of repair. These are bread and butter for any tech and valuable for any touring tech, but they are also very beneficial for the individual guitar owner/player. Learning how to repair your own guitar will not only save you some money but can also be very rewarding. A good knowledge of how to repair an instrument also opens up the world of modification and customising, which all guitarists and guitar owners seem to like to do. This area of work has certainly kept my business very busy for years.

PART ONE

Guitar Setup

CHAPTER 1

Assessment and Understanding the Numbers

Understanding the numbers

As you get started with setting up, maintaining and repairing your own guitars or the guitars of others, you will first need to understand 'the numbers'. These are the measurements – often imperial – that accompany the manufacturers' setup points and tech setup points. Perhaps surprisingly, many of the students who attend our pro setup course do not know that the numbers on packs of strings ('nines', 'tens', and so on) refer to imperial measurements. Buying strings as a kid and even as an adult, before I began my lutherie course, I was unaware of this too. On the other hand, when the students are asked whether they know the difference between a set of 'nines' and a set of 'tens' by feel and by the tension in the strings, they all have an opinion – indeed, they are sometimes quite vocal about it! This is remarkable, since the difference can be as small as one-thousandth of an inch (0.001in) on the High E string – the High E string of a set of 'tens' is 0.010in while a set of 'nines' has a High E string of 0.009in.

Accuracy with the numbers is important. For example, when the optimum

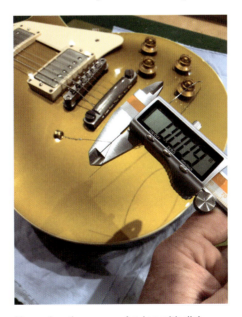

Measuring the gauge of string with dial calipers. Guitar strings are in imperial measurements.

for the neck relief is 0.008in measured at the 7th fret on a 24.75in scale length, the difference will be significant if the neck relief is actually at 0.012in. It will certainly be noticed by the player; whether or not they have a grasp on the specific numbers, they will certainly feel it in the fingers. Although the numbers might be new to you as a builder or repairer, as a player you may already be aware of even very small changes having quite a significant impact on how you enjoy the guitar and its playability.

Style and genre

A player's playing style, in terms of the attack, phrasing and even tone, all come from the setup and this book should help you to reason with this, at least from the point of view of the numbers! An understanding of the numbers and setup points will help you to dial in to what you feel

OPPOSITE: Gibson Les Paul 57 reissue, flat polished and set up – a favourite guitar.

and what you like, how the guitar is in your hands, and how the setup resonates with the guitar. Although the numbers are subjective, as is the feel, assessing and mapping them out makes everything clearer, and will enable you to achieve a setup that gets the best out of the guitar. Often, when we send around the table of six to eight students on our setup course a Gibson Les Paul after messing about with the setup, there will be six to eight different opinions of how it plays and feels. There are also always differences in the descriptions or terminology that the students use. It is the job of a good tech to translate, transpose or interpret the words that are used by a player whose guitar is not quite set up to perfection.

The player's style is certainly relevant when it comes to getting the best setup on the guitar. Setting up a guitar to suit a certain genre can also be an interesting process. It is quite common for guitarists to play in many different styles, so the majority of setups are designed to suit a broad cross-section of music. However, when setting up for jazz, for example, for a player who is really getting into that genre, the setup can be approached a little differently. For this style of play, the guitar does not need much relief in the neck to accommodate a heavy open attack, or much height in the strings to get behind, in order to make big bends, as a heavy blues player might wish to do. A jazz player will be playing more notes and will therefore need the setup to be as quick and easy to play around the open-chord position as much as the higher register. This requires a straighter neck and lower string height.

A blues player tends to attack the open strings a little more than a jazz player, which requires a touch more relief. They may also need to get under the strings

a little more for some tone bends and beyond. Sometimes, if the action height is too low, the player will not be able to experience the feel of getting under the string. Playing country with some nice twangy open-chord runs also requires more relief in the neck, to allow for some bends around the 2nd and 4th fret areas, as well as a fairly low action for some chicken picking.

Having said all that, I have done work for casual jazz players who love a straight neck with a low action height across the whole fretboard, as well as extremely seasoned jazz players who need a bit of a 'fight' with the guitar, otherwise they find the playing too easy and get lazy! Each to their own, as they say. What is clear is that taking your own style into consideration when playing with your setup is very worthwhile. Similarly, when working on a guitar for another person, having an understanding of their style of play, and making an effort to interpret their needs and wishes, is paramount in getting the setup right. Sometimes, your depth of understanding will lead to a

guitar playing better than its owner ever thought possible.

Setup points

The setup points show the parameters of neck relief, where you would try to dial in the setup according to the player's style. A lower amount of neck relief would suit a lighter, more balanced attack; the highest amount of relief on the setup points would be more suitable to a player with a heavier attack. When neither the customer nor the tech knows where the setup works best, and where it may need to cover a number of different styles of play, the tried and tested pro-bench setup is right in the middle of the lowest and highest amount of relief. This enables you to get the guitar feeling good and can be dialed in a little more with a minimal neck relief adjustment of tightening or loosening. Often, being in the middle of those numbers feels great and is well received.

Measuring neck relief using a notched straight edge.

Below are some easily sourced references from Gibson and Fender, covering many of their guitars. Your guitar will not necessarily come to you from the manufacturer with these setup points, as it is likely to have been through a few distribution channels as well as a shop, and the points may have been tweaked or may have changed in transit. The factory specs are simply a guide as to where the manufacturer sees the setup. They differ slightly from the bench setup points, as they are more a range of parameters to be referenced with consideration of the player's styles as well as experience.

Setup points assessment and order of adjustment

Assessing the current setup of a guitar and mapping out the numbers is a great place to start. The process will often highlight a potential issue with the current setup and give you a reference point from which to begin. Many people who try to do their own setup omit to record the setup points and often try to head straight to the issue they are experiencing. A good way to avoid this is to follow the six points of setup assessment and adjustment (*see* below), which lead on to the six points of maintenance. Following these steps really helps keep things in order. Measuring all the points and then adjusting them in the same order every time enables you to see the knock-on effects of any changes, which can be negative if approached in the wrong order.

1. Tune up. This has to be at the pitch of the player. If their guitar needs to be set up at E flat, then the assessment and adjustments all need to be done at that pitch. If you set the guitar up at standard pitch and then the customer plays a semi-tone down, the neck relief and tension in the guitar will change and the setup will be a little wasted, plus the knock-on effects will be significant.

Gibson Electrics Factory Specs

Neck relief	0.012in at 7th fret
Action height bass side	5/64in
Action height treble side	3/64in
Action height 1st fret	0.030in–0.015in
Pickup height neck pickup	3/32in bass and treble
Pickup height bridge pickup	1/16in bass and treble

Fender Electrics Factory Specs

Neck relief	0.012in at 7th fret
Action height bass side	3/32in
Action height treble side	2/32in
Action height 1st fret	0.020in (+/- 0.002in)
Bridge height (lift)	1/32in–4/32in
Pickup heights*	4/32in bass and 3/32in treble

*String fretted at the 21st fret

Bench specs

Fixed Bridge

Relief at 7th fret	0.004in–0.012in
Action height at 12th bass	5/64in
Action height at 12th treble	2/32in
Action height nut to 1st fret	0.016in–0.020in

Floating bridge

Relief at 7th fret	0.006in–0.012in
Action height at 12th bass	5/64in
Action height at 12th treble	2/32in
Action height nut to 1st fret	0.016in–0.020in
Saddle radius	7.25in 9.5in 10in 12in
Floating bridge lift	1/32in–4/32in

Bass

Relief at 7th fret	0.008in–0.016in
Action height at 12th bass	4/32in +/-
Action height at 12th treble	3/32in +/-
Action height nut to 1st fret	0.020in +/-

Tuning up to the correct pitch of the player is vital.

2. Measure the neck relief. It is always good practice to record the exact amount of neck relief once at pitch. There are a couple of ways to do this, but it is highly recommended that you use a notched straight edge and feeler gauges (*see* Chapter 2).

3. Measure the action heights, nut to 1st fret and 12th fret. Use a 6in steel rule with 32nds and 64ths marked on it; most have millimetres marked on the other side too. Feeler gauges for the nut to 1st fret.

4. Measure the saddle radius (for six individual saddle bridges and three saddles on Teles). Assessing this can highlight where the individual string height is a little low. The saddles must mirror the radius of the fretboard (*see* Chapter 4).

5. Measure the float (lift) of the bridge. It is vital to take this measurement before any work is done, as it will certainly change significantly when other areas are adjusted.

6. Assess the intonation. This can be assessed prior to any setup work but it is a little pointless if any of the above setup points are not right, as any change will affect the intonation. This will always be the last thing that will be adjusted and in the playing position.

- Setup Points

① 10 – 2

0.004" - 0.012"	0.024"	0.018"
5/64"	3/32"	
2/32"	2/32"	
0.016" - 0.020"	0.022"	

0.006" - 0.012"
5/64"
2/32"
0.016" - 0.020"
7.25" 9.5" 10" 12"
1/32" - 4/32"

0.008" - 0.012"
3/32" +/-
2/32" +/-
0.016" - 0.020"

The setup points should be assessed and mapped out throughout the process.

Order of maintenance points

With all the setup points assessed and recorded on a setup points sheet (*see* below), the adjustments can begin. However, if the strings on the guitar are old and dirty it is advisable to remove them and do the maintenance side of the setup first. Once the strings are back on and to pitch, the setup adjustments can begin. With the same gauge string going back on the guitar the setup points should be exactly the same. Taking a little time to stretch in the strings will help get the tension right more quickly and make it easier to get to the final setup.

1. Fretboard cleaning. Unfinished boards of rosewood, ebony, and so on, can be cleaned up very well by gently using 0000-grade wire wool and some wood oil soap. Finished fretboards can be cleaned using a clean cloth and a pump polish.
2. Fret polishing. The frets can be polished to a nice shine using a fretboard guard, removing any tarnishing with 0000-grade wire wool or some micromesh papers.
3. Cleaning the electrics. Cleaning the pots well removes and reduces the build-up of dirt in the post and switch, which can cause crackling.

4. Other areas. With the strings off, it is a good opportunity to clean all the areas that are not usually accessible. A clean cloth or disposable fine towels are best.
5. Re-stringing. Once the setup and clean-up have been done, a new set of strings is called for. Stringing back up is another key point in the maintenance regime.
6. Check the pickup heights. Checking the pickup heights is the last item on the list. For manufacturers' specs and ways to measure them, *see* Chapter 12.

Having a starting point and an end goal

Mapping out the setup points helps in numerous ways. If you are a beginner, it will give you confidence in understanding the numbers. They will often indicate that something is not quite right with the setup, and they also give you a good marker for reference. Continuing to map out the numbers and increments as they change will also help if you need to go back a few steps, if the guitar does not feel quite right. I have found that students on our setup course who are already setting up their guitars rarely map out where their starting point is. Often, they are not clear about their end goal either. They know something

is not right with the guitar and they are just going to fix it! Following all the steps of assessment and maintenance will be much more productive and having a good written record can really help with this.

Mapping out the numbers as well as recording the final setup points, including the steps taken to get there, is particularly important when working on guitars that belong to other people. When I first started the repair business I offered a courier service via the website – the owner could book their guitar in and a courier would collect it and deliver it to me. Once the setup was complete, the guitar would be packed up and shipped back. Occasionally – usually when the weather was bad – the customer would call and say the guitar was buzzing and that the neck looked too straight. As I had a written record of how the guitar had been when it left me, I could reassure them that the relief (which had probably changed in transit) had been a particular number, and that the guitar would most likely settle down once it had reacclimatised. I remember a very nice Telecaster having this exact issue. I reassured the customer that the relief had been exactly 0.008in when it left the workshop, suggested leaving the guitar overnight and checking it after 24 hours. Sure enough, he called the next day to tell me it was playing like a dream!

CHAPTER 2

Neck Relief and How to Adjust

Neck relief and truss rods

The term 'neck relief' refers to the bow in the neck of the guitar, which is controlled by the truss rod. The elliptical pattern of the vibrating strings is accommodated by this slight curve in the neck. Positive relief is the pulling up of the neck, and this is more common than negative relief, where the neck is bowing back. Negative relief usually causes some 'fret buzz', as the strings around the open-chord position and up to the 5th fret are closest to the frets. With the strings at tension there is a natural pull on the neck. The truss rod fitted inside a channel in the neck is there to control this.

The neck relief is measured at the 7th fret, the position in the neck that is most important in accommodating the elliptical pattern of the strings. Imagine playing a G note off the 3rd fret of the Bass E; the position where the string is moving the most will be around the 7th to 9th fret.

A guitar needs relief in the neck not only to accommodate the movement of the string but also to reduce the tension over the guitar and add feel and playability. A very straight neck, with a bow of less than 0.004in, will feel tighter than one with, say, 0.012in with the same gauge strings on. That tension with the same gauge strings on the guitar will also differ with different scale lengths – a 24.75in and

Whether it is dual-action or single-action, the truss rod is there to control neck relief. This Gibson has a single-action rod.

OPPOSITE: A great guitar: a Fender custom shop '52 reissue.

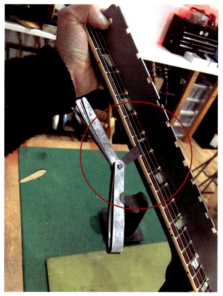

Measuring the neck relief at the 7th fret, using feeler gauges and a notched straight edge.

Gibson with a scale length of 24.75in.

Gibson ⁵⁄₁₆in truss rod at the 10 o'clock position.

Gibson ⁵⁄₁₆in truss rod at the 2 o'clock position.

for the longer scale, 25.5in, are between 0.006in and 0.012in. This is just a little reminder of the fact that the scale is longer, and the tension will be higher in the string naturally, so reducing the neck relief below the start point might result in too high a tension in the string and therefore less feel. However, it is certainly possible and can sometimes suit a player to have that high a tension and the relief to fall below the lower parameter of 0.006in.

The truss rod is placed inside a channel routed in the neck and usually the fretboard is glued on after. The truss rod nut is accessed at the headstock, just past the nut in almost all cases, although on vintage-style Fenders and some derivatives it is located at the heel end of the neck where it joins the body. There are two types of truss rod: single-action and dual-action. The single-action rod can be tightened to reduce the relief and, when it is slackened off, the strings will naturally pull the neck back into relief. With a dual-action truss rod there is tension in the rod. Tightening it will reduce relief and then loosening it will put more relief in the neck by putting pressure on it.

Many people are overly cautious about adjusting the neck relief, for fairly good reasons. However, adjusting the truss rod and the neck relief is more important than anything else in guitar setup, the rest is really just maintenance!

Guitarists and owners often say that they can adjust everything on their guitar except the neck relief and then the truss rod adjustment. Sadly, these are the two actions that are vital for getting the best out of a guitar. The neck relief and adjustment of the truss rod will in turn have a knock-on effect on pretty much all the setup points. A straighter neck will reduce the action height – the string height from the top of the fret to the underside of the

a 25.5in will feel different with the same gauge – and adjusting the neck relief can even that out. An obvious choice of two guitars to demonstrate this difference in tension would be a Gibson Les Paul and a Fender Stratocaster, the former being a 24.75in scale and the latter a 25.5in scale.

This is why neck relief amounts may differ for the two guitars even if they are strung up with strings of the same gauge.

The spec sheet shows that the parameters of neck relief for the shorter of the two scales are between 0.004in and 0.012in (factory spec), whereas the parameters string. A reduction in the neck relief will also alter the nut to 1st fret height as well as the intonation either over the nut to 1st fret, as well as at the 12th fret, where the octave is measured and intonated. With a floating tremolo guitar, a significant reduction in neck relief could also change the float of the bridge with the increase in tension over the string.

Because of all this, it makes no sense when owners tell me that they have set their guitar up really well, but have not yet adjusted the truss rod, and ask me to adjust the neck for them. If I were to do this, it would put out all the setup points they have painstakingly worked on! This is a good reminder of the importance of the order of assessment and adjustment, which is often misunderstood or ignored. Although many players and owners feel they know what is wrong with the guitar and its setup, and will pass this on to the repairer or tech, the worst thing for the repairer or tech to do is to go straight to the problem the owner has suggested and make that one adjustment without checking all the setup points in order and then adjusting them in that order. The first action should always be to make a note of the setup numbers and create a record of the starting point.

As most owners are reluctant to go anywhere near neck relief and truss rod adjustment, there is a tendency to adjust as much of the rest of the setup as possible, to try to get around the problem. In doing this, they are avoiding the area they need to adjust the most. A good example of this, which will also demonstrate the impact of the neck relief, is when an owner says the nut is cut too high. The result is that the distance from the 1st fret to the underside of the string is high, causing intonation issues over the nut, with the string having to travel further to reach the 1st fret. The

angle at which it leads off that fret creates a note that is sharper than it should be (and than it would be, were that angle shallower). It would be extremely unwise to file or sand the nut height down to a desired or correct measurement from factory specs, or otherwise, without first checking the neck relief. With a natural tendency for the neck relief to increase over time, due to the constant tension in the area, it is quite likely that the relief has become more positive since the guitar's most recent setup, string change, and so on. If a more positive neck relief is creating a higher nut to 1st fret height, the string has to travel further down to the 1st fret, which essentially lengthens the scale length to the 1st fret. This will create a sharper note across all the strings.

A simple tightening of the truss rod will reduce the neck relief, straightening the neck and in turn bringing the nut to 1st fret height down. If that falls below 0.020in, then the intonation of the notes will be in a much better position, creating a more in-tune fretted 1st-fret note as well as improving tuning across the open-chord positions.

As well as making an accurate note of the starting point – not by guessing or eyeballing it – it is important to map out the increments of any adjustments. Recording the increments as you go will enable you to head back to a point of neck relief if the final amount does not quite feel right. It can also give the inexperienced person confidence in making adjustments, as they can clearly see the progress and the way back if required.

It might be possible to see what needs to be done by sighting down the neck. If you can see the neck pulling up a little as you focus up and towards the nut area, and can identify a slight curve, the relief

is positive. The opposite, negative relief, is usually even easier to see, with the neck bowing down. The more obvious indication of negative relief, though, is the strings being very close to the fretboard around the 3rd to 5th fret area as you look down the neck. They are often buzzing too.

Methods of measuring

The best place to start is to measure the neck relief accurately, which must always be done at the correct pitch of the player. There are a few methods, but the best one uses a notched straight edge that sits on the fretboard, with the notches between the frets. A feeler gauge is then placed between the fretboard and the notched edge. The neck relief is measured at the 7th fret, which is approximately halfway between the nut and the body join and the area that is referred to as the 'tongue' of the fretboard, which is usually flat and without relief. This area is also where the neck relief needs to accommodate the most movement in the strings.

To take the measurement, hold the neck of the guitar in your hand and use the notched straight edge on the fretboard between the D and G strings, held by thumb and forefinger at the end of the rule. The guitar should be off the neck support or bench, particularly if it is heavy, as a guitar at rest on the bench might indicate more relief due to the weight. Slide different feeler gauges between the gap where you can see light at the 7th fret. When the feeler gauge is touching both the fretboard and the underside of the notched straight edge, the amount of relief in the neck can be measured. If the notched straight edge makes a knocking sound as you remove the feeler gauge, the feeler gauge is too large and therefore the relief is less. Keep going until the contact is good between feeler gauge, fretboard and rule, and when there is no light visible at the fret.

Another way to assess a guitar's neck relief is to use a capo on the 1st fret and then fret the last fret with your right hand making the string the straight edge. Carefully placing a feeler gauge under the string and over the fret at the 7th fret will give you the same neck relief reading. It does require a steady hand and can be a bit awkward, but it is a useful method for a tech who is on the go at a gig without all their tools. There is usually a capo close to hand.

'Sighting' the neck is another way to gauge neck relief. Having shown and taught this over the years, however, I have come to the conclusion that everyone's eyes are different – and that they change over time! Sighting the neck is therefore recommended only as a way of deciding simply whether the neck is in relief or not. Ascertaining a measurement by eye is very tricky and even after years of experience an educated guess would be the best you could expect to achieve.

For someone who is planning to open a repair shop and set up guitars professionally, there are tools such as neck jigs, which can give even more accurate measurements and help with emulating neck relief. They are quite expensive, however, and a notched straight edge and some feeler gauges will work very well for most people. The notched straight edge I bought in 2007, for six-string electric scales and bass scales, is still in service daily. Buy the best-quality tools you can afford, and you should only need to buy them once.

Having and knowing parameters is a good place to start. These can be referenced either from manufacturers' specifications or from the bench specs given here (*see* Chapter 1). These are generally quite similar, with subtle differences that reflect differing scales. They are only a guide and once you are more familiar with accurately measuring and adjusting neck relief you will be able to work out a more tailored set of parameters that suit both you and the guitar, as well as the owner's playing style. By continually improving your understanding of this area, you will be better able to individually dial in the best setup. Working to the bench or manufacturers' specs is a great place to start and will serve you well for some time, or indeed throughout your ownership. However, with a more informed and more confident approach you can achieve a more fulfilled setup experience. One tip to get closer to your ideal neck relief setup is to measure one of your guitars that has always felt great to play – maybe it came from the shop like this or it has recently been set up by a great tech. Measure the neck relief and see how it sits within the parameters. This could indicate a personal preference for having the neck at that amount on that specific scale length with that gauge of string. It might also show you that there could be room for improvement.

Becoming familiar with this area of adjustment and setup is totally key to getting the best out of your guitar. With practice, some guidelines, parameters to work to and confidence, you will be able to get a guitar to play extremely well.

Natural changes

Neck relief is the main area in the electric guitar that can change of its own accord. This can happen due to alterations in temperature or humidity, a change of string gauge and even a change to the pitch of the guitar. A higher gauge and higher pitch both lead to more tension, which will increase the relief in the neck.

This natural change in the neck relief is another reason why it is important to record the amount that the guitar has when the setup has been completed, especially if the guitar is heading back out on tour or being couriered back to its owner. Sometimes, perhaps in transit or between the bench and the stage, there can be differences in temperature and/or humidity that may be sufficient to alter the neck relief. An accurate record of the setup that existed at the point at which the guitar left the bench will be helpful in the event of any environmental change or movement. The tech will be able to reassure the owner that the setup was right when it left the workshop, and that the neck should settle back to where it was as soon as it has acclimatised.

The truss rod: access and adjustment

Accessing the truss rod:

On most guitars, the truss rod is located at the headstock end of the neck. On most Fender-style guitars there is a small opening that shows the truss rod end just under the nut. This type of rod is often adjusted using a small Allen key, in metric or imperial, depending on where the guitar was made. The majority of Fender-style guitars have the truss rod at the headstock end, but vintage Fenders and their re-issues have it located in the butt of the neck. For more on this, *see* 'Alternative Applications', below.

Gibson truss rods are located under a truss rod cover; Gibson guitars have two screws, while Epiphone instruments have three. The Gibson-style truss rod requires a nut wrench (⁵⁄₁₆in), as do PRS and Rickenbacker guitars.

Some manufacturers have developed the truss rod further. Ernie Ball MusicMan guitars' rods are most commonly located at the end of the fretboard. This allows the holed wheel-style end to be very easily turned, tightened or loosened to get the optimum relief.

The relevant Allen keys (metric) or nut wrenches (imperial) are as follows:

- Gibson ⁵⁄₁₆in
- Epiphone 5mm or 7mm
- Fender USA ⅛in
- Fender Mexico ³⁄₁₆in
- PRS ⁵⁄₁₆in
- PRS SE 8mm
- Rickenbacker ¼in
- Ibanez 7mm (RG/JEM) or 8mm
- Gretsch USA and Japan ⁵⁄₁₆in
- Gretsch Electromatic 4mm

When starting out I purchased two full sets of Allen keys in metric and imperial from Machine Mart and those covered pretty much all the Allen key slotted truss rods. There are a few UK and US suppliers for the nut wrenches, including WD Music, All Parts and StewMac. Most guitar manufacturers now supply the relevant wrenches and Allen keys, but there was a time when you were lucky if you got anything extra in the case.

Adjusting the truss rod

First, measure and record the amount of neck relief, along with the other setup points, action height, nut to 1st fret

Truss-rod adjustment can be done with a nut wrench or an Allen key.

height, and the float of the tremolo, if applicable. These can all change with a truss rod adjustment so having them all mapped out beforehand will help flag up any knock-on effects, and in some cases remove the need to address any of the

heights that are not correct. Now is also the time to double-check the pitch and make an adjustment.

If the neck has positive relief, this can be reduced by tightening the truss rod. Many people use the terms 'quarter-turn' or 'eighth of a turn' on the truss rod, but it is easier to imagine a clock face when adjusting (clockwise to tighten) and to record the increments accordingly. This will help you gain confidence in locating the starting point of the adjustment, as well as where it is going – usually 10 o'clock to 12 o'clock, or 10 o'clock to 2 o'clock, if the neck relief is significant. This area of adjustment is often concerning for the uninitiated and visualising a clock face can be slightly less subjective than talking about a quarter-turn or an eighth of a turn. In addition, picturing a clock face keeps it nice and simple when you need to remember that you adjust clockwise to tighten and anti-clockwise to loosen.

With the truss rod Allen key or nut wrench placed on the nut at as close to 10 o'clock as possible, proceed to tighten,

Tightening the truss rod will reduce the neck relief.

clockwise, to 12 o'clock and then re-tune. If the relief has measured at twice the amount referenced by either the bench specs or manufacturers' specs, this turn of the truss rod could be increased from 10 o'clock to 12 o'clock to 10 o'clock to 2 o'clock on the clock face.

For the novice, proceeding in smaller increments will reduce any fear of going too far too quickly and creating a problem. It will also allow you to prove the concept of adjusting your own neck relief safely.

With any adjustment made to the truss rod, the strings will be affected – they will be slightly sharp if the neck relief has been reduced by a tightening (clockwise turn) of the truss rod, or slightly flat if the truss rod has been slackened off (anti-clockwise). The string tension must be brought back to pitch before measuring again and seeing where the neck relief now sits. This slackening off and bringing the strings back up to pitch will also settle the neck relief; the adjustment and change are that swift on pretty much all electric guitars. Remember to always flatten the notes and bring them back up to pitch. This always helps settle the string and results in a more stable string as well as an accurate neck relief measurement.

Hopefully, with the initial tightening of the truss rod (if the neck relief was positive), measuring with the notched straight edge back on the fretboard in the same position between the D and G strings and using the feeler gauges will indicate that the neck relief is less than before. It is difficult to suggest the amount of reduction that will occur with each adjustment – the adjustment is made according to the measurement and to the direction of travel in terms of the numbers wise. Each change should be recorded. Assuming that one '10 to 2' adjustment has caused the neck relief to decrease by 0.006in, leaving the neck relief at 0.020in, two more adjustments

using the same 10 to 2 increment should bring the neck relief in by a further 0.012in, giving an end result of 0.008in.

To assume the change in neck relief is something to steer away from, the adjustment and straightening of the neck is not linear, the thickness of the neck, the fretboard material all combining will reduce the efficiency of the adjustments. It is therefore good practice to measure, make the adjustment and re-measure, and continue on adjusting in small steps, one at a time. On the practical part of the setup course, students are often surprised at how the numbers change and the ways in which the neck relief can reduce. Sometimes an adjustment seems not to do much at all, then the very next adjustment takes in a significant amount of relief. Recording the neck relief at the start and with each increment really helps a student to master this important part of guitar setup.

If the neck relief is negative at the start, which is really uncommon, the truss rod needs to be loosened, with an anti-clockwise adjustment of either '2 to 12' or '2 to 10'. Usually with a guitar that has negative relief a tech will immediately back the truss rod off and rarely bother to record the negative neck relief. However, by placing the notched straight edge between the D and G strings and using a feeler gauge at the 2nd fret, it should be possible to measure with the feeler gauges between the fretboard and the rule.

Once the truss rod has been slackened off and the guitar is back to pitch, it can settle in the rack overnight and be checked the next day to see whether the neck is now in relief. At that point, the relief can be measured in the usual way and then re-set. Negative relief on a guitar is often a result of it having been subjected to a change in temperature or humidity, perhaps when it has been left in a van or

car overnight. The best thing to do is to get that neck back into positive relief.

The effect on the setup and feel

A player's style should always be taken into consideration when adjusting neck relief. If the guitar has minimal relief in the neck, say, less than 0.004in, the string tension will feel quite tight. This might be very good for a seasoned jazz player, a player who will not bend the strings or a player who likes to play with speed, running around the 1st fret to the 5th as efficiently as they do at the 12th to 15th fret area. When the neck is this straight, the strings will naturally be lower to the frets, and a gentle or a considered attack will be required. With this low neck relief, any playing too hard on the strings will more than likely cause some string buzz, particularly off the 1st fret area. The lower the neck relief the lower the nut to first fret height will be, which again could suit a jazz player.

Where there is more relief in the neck – say, 0.008in when measured at the 7th fret – there is more give in the string tension, which allows the string to bend further and with more ease. In this case, the attack of the player can be heavier and, as the nut to 1st fret will be higher too, it is likely that the elliptical pattern of the string will be better accommodated. This amount of relief could suit blues and rock players, as their playing style usually has more attack on the open notes, power chords and bigger bends. Generally, 0.008in is a suitable amount of relief for most players and styles, as it feels good all round. If you are unsure of your own playing style on your own guitar, or the setup needs to cover a lot of genres (very common), this could be a good amount of neck relief to aim for and work with.

A measurement of 0.012in – which is the factory spec for a Gibson Les Paul – would accommodate a heavy attacking style, possibly suitable for a country player. With more relief in the neck and a slightly higher nut to 1st fret measurement, it is good for open chords and playing off the first few frets. The relief should not affect the ability to bend cleanly and with this lower tension over the strings the feel has more ease to it.

Relief that is any higher than 0.012in is not necessarily wrong and may suit an individual with a heavy attack. However, with more upward curve the angles will reduce the higher you go up the board and there will be a time when the neck relief will force a 'choke' on the strings. This happens when a bend is played and as the string heads into the board the note stops ringing out. When dealing with a neck relief of at least 0.012in and even higher, the string height will inevitably be high too and then the tendency would be to lower the bridge height to get a more appealing and more playable string height. This will often compound a playability issue as the curvature of the neck underneath the strings will be quite significant below the 12th fret and the string height will actually be lower around the 12th fret than around the 5th to the 7th fret. Although the strings will feel fairly close to the frets around the lead playing area of the fretboard, 12th and above, they will feel uneven in other areas. Quite often this is noticeable with guitars that have been hanging on a wall in rising heat in a house or shop. The more costly the guitar the higher up the wall it is in the shop, which will usually add more relief. When the guitar setup is eyeballed by the owner or by a staff member in a shop and that string height looks high, the bridge is usually rolled down to make it look better!

Sadly, this compounds the lack of playability. It is a truss rod adjustment that will bring it back to an easy guitar to play.

Dialling in the correct amount of relief, with the feel and style of the player in mind, does take time to get right. Sometimes, an increment of just five minutes (on the imaginary clock), reducing the relief from 0.008in to 0.007in, can feel really great. Most guitar owners and players are likely to have experienced the difference between a set of 9-gauge strings and a set of 10-gauge strings, so they will be well aware of how significant such a tiny measurement as 0.001in can feel! Once you have become more familiar with adjusting your neck relief, it is well worth trying out different amounts. Some players will even change their neck relief each time they pick up the guitar to suit the genre they are playing. The key is to become very comfortable and confident with making adjustments to the relief, so that you can get the feel just right for whatever style you or others choose to play. There is so much confidence to be gained once you have understood and mastered neck relief adjustment, and positive feedback in getting your guitar right.

Case study: Gibson Les Paul standard

The guitar used was a Gibson Les Paul that had 0.022in neck relief at the 7th fret. This amount of relief is quite evident to the naked eye, most noticeably in the middle of the fretboard. Assessing the relief by eye is a good start and the ability to 'sight' the neck develops with experience, but measuring with a notched straight edge is best. This is the only method I have used for well over fifteen years.

Neck relief measured at 0.022in at the 7th fret.

The Gibson Les Paul was at standard pitch with a set of 10-gauge strings on. These were fairly new, so could easily handle the adjustments. Sometimes, if the strings are really old and dirty it may be best to do the maintenance part of the setup first. Remove the strings and perform the clean-up, re-string and settle the strings in with a little stretching (*see* Chapters 10 and 11), then get the guitar to pitch and measure the neck relief.

Measuring the rest of the setup points on this style of guitar – relief, action height at the 12th fret and 1st fret – maps out the numbers enough to see how the guitar is currently set up, as well as providing a reference for how the change in neck relief will alter the other numbers. According to the setup points specs the minimal relief is 0.004in and the max 0.012in, so the target will be 0.008in measured at the 7th fret. This is in the middle of the lower and higher relief amounts and is a level that is proven to cover many genres and to give a very playable amount of relief. It also allows, once the rest of the setup points are accurate, the dialling in of a small amount either side to find the sweet spot. This could require a tightening or loosening of the truss rod of less than a five-minute increment on the imaginary clock face.

With the guitar on the bench and holding the fretboard with the right hand and using the left hand to adjust, the truss rod was adjusted from 10 o'clock to 2 o'clock with a ⁵⁄₁₆in nut wrench. The strings were then returned to pitch and a change of 0.006in relief in the neck was measured at the 7th fret. This new amount was still twice as much as the tried and tested pro bench spec, as per the spec chart, and higher than the manufacturer's neck relief specs too. With this in mind, it should be possible to make the same small adjustment and reduce the relief to a minimum of 0.004–0.006in, or possibly more. The neck relief reduction is not linear and it would be unwise to assume that, because one 10 to 2 adjustment gained 0.006in, another would do exactly the same. Two or three 10 to 2 turns should result in the relief landing on the desired number. The thickness of the neck and the fretboard, and the wood of the fretboard, will all contribute to how the neck pulls in with the adjustments, so it is best to continue to adjust in small increments and then re-tune and record the reduction on a setup points chart.

Making too many adjustments without correcting the string pitch can prove problematic. If the strings are sharpened too much and too quickly with too much tightening, this could cause a string to break, which would in turn alter the tension in the neck quickly and then require that string to be changed and brought up to pitch in order to continue the adjustment. Also, when the truss rod is tightened too many times without addressing the string

pitch, when you come to slacken off and bring back to pitch, the neck will continue to straighten. This may result in too little relief in the neck, potentially creating fret buzz and some cause for concern. It is much better to make smaller adjustments, and more of them, and to be able to see how the neck is coming to you and proving that concept.

After re-tuning and recording the incremental changes on the setup points sheet, the truss rod was adjusted with another 10 to 2 clockwise turn and then a measurement was taken using the notched straight edge between the D and G strings. The measurement was 0.012in at the 7th fret, a reduction in the neck relief of 0.004in, which was now in line with the relief parameters on the setup points specs as well as the manufacturer's specs. (The manufacturer's specs are slightly on the high side compared with most bench and pro specs, as well as most customers' ideal numbers. This can be down to giving the relief a bit more room to accommodate the style of individual players, the manufacturer not knowing who will play their guitar, and so on.) It may be worth seeing how the guitar plays at this stage – getting a feel of the small incremental changes can be very beneficial when learning about neck relief adjustment. If you are familiar with the neck relief amount that you are aiming for, though, you may not want to play it until you reach that measurement.

Once the desired amount of relief is close, it is best to reduce the extent of the turn on the truss rod by half. This means making a 10 to 12 turn instead of a 10 to 2 turn. The neck relief was pulling up by about 0.004in with each adjustment, so you need to go a little more gently. Also, the truss rod is getting very tight, and it is getting harder to do the adjustment with

the ⁵⁄₁₆in wrench. Learn to be aware of how tight the truss rod feels when adjusting. However, if you have a similar amount of relief at this stage, it is certainly within the tolerance of the truss rod and there is some capacity for it to be adjusted further.

The guitar may already be at the correct amount of neck relief, having been set up by the manufacturer or shop, so you need to be confident with the numbers and measure accurately. Just the first turn on the truss rod could get you to the desired number, so going slowly and confidently is key.

With the guitar tuning double-checked, the guitar was re-tuned to pitch. When re-tuning, you need to be aware of the change of pitch on particular strings, as some will sharpen more than others. Any sharpening also demonstrates that the neck is straightening – in other words, it is going the right way.

Having the left hand on the nut wrench and keeping the right hand holding the neck is very important at this stage, as the guitar will easily move off the bench as the truss rod gets tighter and more difficult to turn. The small 10 to 12 clockwise turn may be tough but it is doing exactly what it is designed to do.

After following all the steps of adjustment, the neck relief was measured at 0.008in at the 7th fret with the notched straight edge and feeler gauges.

If the bridge height on this type of guitar is too low, the new amount of relief might cause the string action height to be too low too. If the bridge was in the right place before the adjustments, and the neck relief is now correct, it could be the case that the string action height is exactly where it should be. This proves that the only element that will change of its own accord is the neck relief.

Neck relief measured at 0.08in at the 7th fret after adjustments.

Alternative applications

The truss rod in some vintage Fenders and vintage re-issues (US and Japan) is located in the heel of the neck. Some early Teles had a small rout above the neck pickup that would allow access with a right-angled screwdriver, making it a little easier. This is not the case with all Tele bodies, though.

There are various views as to why Leo Fender decided to locate the access to the truss rod at the heel end of the neck. He may have had concerns about removing wood around the weakest part of the headstock area in order to allow access. Having had to repair many broken Gibson headstocks, I understand this theory – the removal of too much wood in that area could be a contributing factor, although the neck angle on the guitars and the neck being a one-piece item are more than likely the actual reasons.

Another view is that Fender did not want to pay royalties to Gibson for his patent on his style of truss rod access at the headstock end. In the very early 1950s

Adjusting neck relief: step by step

1. Tune the guitar to the correct pitch of the player.
2. Measure the neck relief at the 7th fret with the notched straight edge and feeler gauge off the bench, with the neck in hand.
3. Measure the 12th fret and nut to 1st fret height and make a note for your records.
4. Adjust (by tightening) the truss rod with a 10 to 2 clockwise turn if positive.
5. Re-tune, measure and record the amount of neck relief. Continue if the neck relief is still more than bench or factory specs.
6. Continue to adjust (tighten) with a 10 to 2 clockwise turn.
7. Re-tune, measure and record the amount of neck relief. Continue if the neck relief is still more than bench or factory spec, but halve the increments if you're getting close to the desired amount of neck relief.
8. Tighten the truss rod by half the previous turn, 10 to 12.
9. Re-tune and measure the neck relief.

If the bridge height and therefore string height are good and to numbers, play the guitar and see how it feels. Note the tension in the string, and the playability around open-chord areas and further up the neck. It may be worth considering the intonation at this point in the assessment, now that the neck relief is where it should be.

Fenders did not have a truss rod at all, and they were introduced only because customers were concerned about them not having one. A fabulous Parker Fly on the bench – an amazing guitar with a carbon-fibre neck and fretboard – seemed not to need one. Similarly, Martin guitars did not have truss rods until the mid-1980s. It is clear from earlier examples that they did not really need them either.

As a result, on most Fenders the truss rod is only accessed by tilting the neck at an angle to expose its end, or by removing it, which might be too much to ask for the complete novice. It can be done following a few simple steps and precautions, but it does make adjusting the neck relief slightly more pressured. If the neck has a lot of relief and needs a few adjustments to get it right, this is what you will have to do; ideally, though, you will want to do it only once rather than multiple times!

A top tip here is to use a capo. Usually, the vintage re-issue Fenders that have the truss rod in the heel of the neck will also have vintage-style machine heads. Slackening off the strings can make the strings pop out of the heads, creating even more

Fender vintage-style truss rod in the heel of the neck.

work. With the capo anywhere between the 5th and 9th fret, and obviously after measuring the neck relief accurately and recording that on the setup points page, slowly de-tune each string by at least a few tones. The strings want to be fairly slack so that when you remove the neck they are not pulling up. Another tip would be to count the number of turns you make on the machine heads. This counting of the turns (usually about five or six full turns is enough) allows you to get back close to pitch once the neck is on and takes some time out of the process, especially if you have to carry out the procedure a few times.

With the strings slackened off, and holding the neck on to the body, proceed to slowly loosen the four neck screws. Having the body on the bench at 90 degrees will allow you to handle the neck and body carefully (*see* below).

Remove the screws and neck plate whilst holding the body and neck together, just in case the neck wants to fall out of the pocket, and then slowly get the guitar (body and neck in place) on the bench.

With the neck and body angled over the bench, gently press on the neck around the middle of the fretboard. The neck should move in the neck pocket, exposing the truss rod end, which is usually slotted. Use a large Phillips screwdriver to make your adjustment – clockwise to tighten the truss rod, reducing the neck relief, and anti-clockwise to put some more relief in the neck. Try to be as accurate as you can with the adjustment. This will come with time and experience so that you will be able to land exactly where you want to be in terms of neck relief. It is very normal to have to do the whole procedure a couple of times to achieve exactly the right neck relief.

With the adjustment made, the neck needs to be carefully pushed back down into the neck pocket and the neck plate and screws put back and tightened fully with the guitar back on the bench at 90 degrees. With the guitar back on the bench and neck support, proceed to re-tune (counting the machine head turns). Once you have the guitar back to the correct pitch, you can re-measure the neck relief.

Hopefully it will be where you want it to be or what you were aiming for. You will not be able to judge fully whether the amount of neck relief is right until the rest of the setup points have been adjusted. Fingers crossed it will be. If not, the entire process will have to be re-done.

One customer had a fantastic '53 Relic Telecaster with a truss rod at the heel end. After about a year of playing the setup had changed and, as is common, the neck relief had pulled from a good 0.008in at the 7th fret to about 0.014in at the 7th. That was pretty standard for a year of playing, changes in temperature, and so on. Having followed all the steps to remove the neck to expose the truss rod, I tightened the end by a 10 to 2 turn, which felt quite tight, and then proceeded to get the neck back in the pocket and the guitar back to pitch.

The neck relief was actually a little lower than it had been before the change, from a setup the year before. It was only 0.006in at the 7th fret. I thought this would be OK, so I carried on with getting the rest of the setup points in and maintenance jobs done, and finally re-stringing the guitar with some fresh strings. Once the strings had settled and I was able to really get digging into the playability I knew that the neck was a touch too straight. It felt tight and not very giving. Getting that lovely Telecaster twang and those country licks around the 2nd to 4th frets was difficult and I could not quite get underneath the string enough. It just did not have that awesome feel that had been so apparent when it had well set up. It could not be ignored and left; the neck just had to come off and the truss rod backed off a little. With the strings slackened and the capo on, and the neck screws and plate off, I did a very small (12 to 11) turn loosening the truss rod. With the screws and plate back on and the strings back to pitch, the neck

Removing the neck screws to be able to pitch the neck back to adjust the truss rod.

Vintage-style truss-rod adjustment at the 10 o'clock position.

Vintage style truss-rod adjustment at the 12 o'clock position.

Vintage-style truss-rod adjustment at 2 o'clock.

relief was measuring 0.008in and the feel of that guitar was back! The open-chord position playing and the bends around that area felt great, and I could get behind the string enough. Further up the fretboard it felt easy and super playable. Sometimes and after years of setup you just know you are going to have to re-do the painstaking work to get the guitar just right.

Although I remember that particular guitar and the process very well, the same has happened with many other examples. Knowing how to 'dial in' to each guitar to get the best out of it comes with experience. It may be relatively quick and easy, or it may be painstaking, but with every guitar there is an opportunity to learn. There was also a reminder here that that there can be a noticeable change in feel with the smallest difference in neck relief. Remember, most players are able to discern the difference between a set of 8s and a set of 10s. On the High E string that difference is just 0.002in, the same as the difference in the '53 Relic Tele's neck relief.

Most Rickenbackers have two truss rods, allowing an adjustment of the amount of relief on both the bass side and the treble side. Pre-1980s ones are supposedly not very strong so it is wise to go gently with an early Ricky. There might be an argument for making any adjustment to the truss rod when the guitar is not fully at pitch, doing the adjustment and then bringing it back to pitch to see whether it is back in line and at desired specs. Modern examples, from the mid-1980s onwards, are more robust. I have always found them to be good for getting the neck relief controlled. A lovely Fireglow 360 came into the workshop some years ago after being leant up against a radiator during the summer and then sadly left there when the central heating went back on. The neck relief was huge – probably an eighth of an inch. I adjusted both truss rods a couple of 10 to 2 turns (tightening) each day over the course of a week, every time just re-tuning the guitar after the adjustment and then letting it settle. It took six days to get it back to specs! It all worked out and the owner was delighted.

CHAPTER 3

String Height Action

Understanding string heights

The term 'action' refers to the height of the string from the top of the fret. The action height plays a significant role in how the guitar plays and feels, as well as affecting the tone of the guitar. There is a common assumption that it is better for the string height to be as low as possible, but this can actually impede the tone. In the same way as the neck relief accommodates the movement of the moving string, the action will influence playability and tone. Again, it is important to be aware of the playing style of the owner: heavy attacking, using a pick or not, or gentler.

The nut to first fret height also needs to be considered in relation to the overall action and playability. This height is set at the factory and is influenced significantly by the neck relief. In the order of assessment and adjustment, the string height is always recorded at the 12th fret and the 1st, the 12th with a rule and usually in ³⁄₃₂in, and the nut to 1st in thousandths of an inch. It is rare that the nut will need to be filed to bring the height in; this is usually covered by any truss rod adjustment and very minimally by setting the bridge height

in order to get the action at the 12th as desired. For issues with the nut that are over and above setup work, *see* Part 3.

Measuring the action at the 12th fret and 1st fret

Using a 6in steel rule placed on the top of the 12th fret, measure up to the bottom

of the string. On the bass side, the measurement with the Bass E string is approximately ³⁄₃₂in (2.4mm) and on the Treble E, commonly ²⁄₃₂in (1.6mm).

As the action height is influenced greatly by the neck relief, before adjusting the action height it is important to get the neck relief correct or as desired. This also applies to the nut to 1st fret heights. To measure the nut to 1st fret height, use a feeler gauge placed underneath the strings and on top

Measuring 12th fret action height, bass side.

OPPOSITE: A 1963 Gibson ES335, restored a few years ago and still regularly serviced in the workshop.

Measuring 12th fret action height, treble side.

Measuring 12th fret action height, Gibson-style bass side.

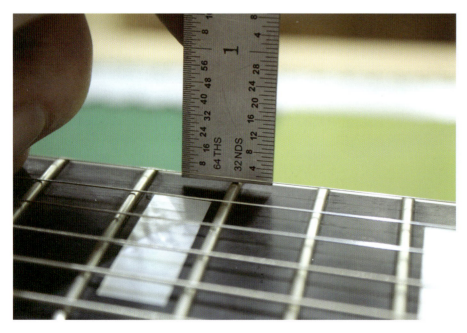

Measuring 12th fret action height, Gibson-style treble side.

of the 1st fret, putting in a little radius to match the radius of the fret and fretboard.

It is sometimes easier to measure the nut to 1st fret height using the feeler gauges approaching from the bass side, under the E, A and D strings and then approaching from the treble side, under the E, B and G. The nut to 1st fret height should be between 0.016in and 0.020in; if it is any lower than this, the strings will vibrate and touch that 1st fret, causing some open string buzz. If it is higher than 0.020in, the notes played over the nut and the first few frets will be sharper, giving the impression that the open-chord intonation of the guitar is out. Your neck relief measurement should reassure you about the nut to 1st fret – if you have a lot of relief then the nut to 1st fret height will more than likely be high. The opposite will be true, too – with no relief, the nut to 1st fret height will be low.

Action height (string height) alternative

Reading the 6in steel rule often causes confusion. Some people find it very difficult to see the relevant line on the rule to the underside of the string and may need help to 'get their eye in'. The trick is to

Measuring nut to 1st fret height, with the feeler gauge over the fret and under the string.

understand that the gap above the string to the line is equal to the space between the two lines below. Alternatively, you can try to look at both the 3/32nd side as well as the 64th side of the rule and get to the height that way.

Eyesight changes over time, with short-sightedness becoming long-sightedness, and so on. Some older students and customers do struggle with measuring the exact action height accurately and have to rely on gauging it by eye or trying to establish a feel of where the height of the string needs to be. This can take a lot of practice, but it should come with experience. In contrast, measuring the neck relief accurately with a notched straight edge and some feeler gauges is usually well understood and carried out with relative ease. The nut to 1st fret height is also relatively easy to measure using feeler gauges, although sometimes it needs to be reiterated that some radius should be put in the gauge if checking the nut to 1st fret distance across the entire fret.

In the factory specs and the bench specs, the action height is given as a fraction, but this can be easily converted into decimal. The action height is therefore measured in a similar way to the relief and the nut to 1st fret height, using feeler gauges. Usually, the set of feeler gauges has about 25 sleeves, the largest being 0.025in, then 0.024in, all the way down to 0.001in. Adding three or four of these first few larger feeler gauges will get you to between 0.075in and 0.095in with ease, adding or subtracting a few to get to the desired measurement. (The decimalisation chart below should cover all the factory and bench specs for action height.)

For an action height of 3/32in on the bass side you can get 0.093in feeler gauges together and check to see whether the group of feeler gauges fit between the top of the fret and the string. If there is a gap and 3/32in is the desired action height (once the neck relief is correct), the bridge saddle or thumb wheel can be lowered

until the string meets the feeler gauges. If the feeler gauges move the string up, then the bridge saddle or thumb wheel will need to be raised slightly. This should then be applied to the treble side, starting with fewer feeler gauges as the treble side is always a lower action height. Remove some feeler gauges to get to 0.062in (2/32in) and then check from the top of the fret to the underside of the string. As is the case with the nut to 1st fret height measuring, this does require a steady hand and you need to take care not to move the strings, but it does remove the uncertainty of how each individual's eyes see it.

For ease, if you have a set of dial calipers you can easily bunch together a few feeler gauges and then press the dial calipers on to them and get a reading of how much they are combined. Remember this is only for the outer E strings. With a fixed bridge-style guitar (Les Paul and all derivatives) we measure the outer E and the internal four strings in the bridge are fixed, already set to the radius of the fretboard. With individual saddle bridges (Strats, Teles, and so on), the outer Es are adjusted in this way until they are correct and then a radius gauge is used to get the remaining strings proportional height correct.

Decimalisation chart

(Numerator/denominator,
for example = 3/32)
4/32in = 0.125in
7/64in = 0.109in
3/32in = 0.093in
5/64in = 0.078in
2/32in = 0.062in
3/64in = 0.046in
1/32in = 0.031in

This method helps students to get to the desired action height more quickly and with less reliance on their eyes. Some can still see the line of 32nds or 64ths well, but it is worthwhile becoming familiar with getting the feeler gauges measured with the dial calipers and checking the action height that way.

Different types of bridge and their adjustment

Fixed bridge (most commonly Gibson style)

Fixed bridges usually have two mounting studs, bass and treble. The Gibson ABR 1 has two ⁵⁄₃₂in threaded rods screwed directly into the body with two thumb wheels that can be turned to raise or lower the bridge. This was designed by Gibson's Ted McCarty in 1953 for the Super 400 and then used for the Les Paul Custom in 1954.

The symmetrical design of the bridge can be placed either way around on the two posts. The ABR1 was originally intended to have the screws for each individual saddle facing the neck and bridge pickup.

Gibson's other style of bridge was a modern replacement for the ABR1, when Gibson moved to Nashville from Kalamazoo. Known as the Nashville Tune O Matic, it has the stud and thumb wheel fitted into the body and cast directly on to the bridge. It is slightly wider, for better intonation, and sturdier.

It is not uncommon to see marks under the bridge and around the thumb wheels where people have tried to adjust this style of bridge – not the done thing on a pro's bench! The multi-spanner is a great little tool for adjusting either style of bridge. It makes it easy to turn the thumb wheels and reduces the risk of marking the top of the guitar.

After any adjustment, raising or lowering the bridge, the guitar must be re-tuned back to the pitch of the player. If the bridge has been raised, the strings will be sharp and have more tension in them, which will in turn create a touch more neck relief. As a result, the strings' tuning must always be settled and brought back to pitch.

Epiphone's bridges are very similar but, on nearly all of them, the two slot heads are slotted so that a screwdriver can be used to turn them, to raise or

Gibson ABR bridge. Adjusting the action height with a multi-spanner.

Epiphone Tune O Matic bridge with flat head adjustment.

style locked on to the bridge posts, the grub screws must be slackened off before adjusting the height.

Some Gretsch guitars have an Adjusto-Matic style bridge on top of a wooden base, which is sometimes pinned to the top of the guitar. This is more common on the more modern Gretsches. *See* Chapter 6 on intonation for how best to locate the unpinned bridges.

Fender Stratocasters can also have fixed bridges, the 'hard-tail' Strat, which is fairly rare. Fender's Telecaster is also a fixed bridge in that they don't have any float. Both of these 'fixed' bridges are adjusted by raising their individual saddles, covered in the next section. Usually, there are two grub screws per saddle that can be raised or lowered with a small Allen key.

Floating bridges – individual saddles

Individual-saddled bridges are often associated with Fenders and all the other similar manufacturers. They usually have six saddles and were originally designed for better intonation. The height of each individual saddle can be set to match the fretboard radius.

To get the desired action height, the outer E strings are raised or lowered to the action height measured at the 12th fret, the same way as with the fixed bridge. To get the other saddles to the correct height, it is necessary to radius the saddles to mirror the fretboard radius. (*See* Chapter 4 for more on saddle radiusing.)

The action height on a Floyd Rose bridge can be adjusted in a similar way to a fixed bridge, by turning the two posts on which the front of the bridge rests. Most can be done with an Allen key, while others have a slotted head for a screwdriver. Again,

lower the action height of both bass and treble. This makes the adjustment a little easier and means that there is less risk of marking the top. However, if the studs are done up really tight, it can be easy to burr the top. In the worst case, the screwdriver can slip out of the slot and cause damage to the top of the guitar.

There are plenty of after-market variations of these bridges, one of which is TonePros', which uses small grub screws to 'lock in' the bridge against the posts. The pinned-in bridge was designed for better tonal response and is also helpful when changing strings, and keeping the bridge set at the current height. When working on a TonePros bridge or similar with the measurement taken at the 12th fret and the neck relief correct, you can raise or lower the bass or treble side. For more on Floyd Rose bridges, *see* Chapter 5.

Pitching the neck using a shim

Another way to reduce the action height on a bolt-on style guitar and one that does not usually have any pitch in the neck (the angle into the body being zero) is to pitch the neck back. This then enables you to raise the saddles. It is very useful when all the saddles on the bridge are as low as they can go, and the grub screws are protruding out of the saddles. These can be sharp and impede the player.

Remove the neck as if adjusting a truss rod that is located in the heel end of the neck. With a capo on, slacken the strings, undo and remove the three or four neck screws and gently push down on the neck, releasing the neck from the pocket. For years, shims have been used to gain better break angle. After taking apart and photographing one 1960 Fender Strat in the workshop, I discovered a small dark red thin shim inside the neck pocket. After a little bit of research, I found photos from the 1950s showing these factory shims. It was a clear clue to the authenticity of that guitar, along with the combined output of the pickups, which were late 1959. A shim can really help get the action height correct and the saddles in a better place, so that the player cannot feel the grub screws.

With individual saddles, the outer E string saddles are adjusted first.

Fender's Micro-Tilt system on a 1970s Stratocaster.

– usually quite dramatically – and that the saddles all now need raising. Starting with the outer E strings, get them back up to required measurements, $\frac{3}{32}$in on the bass and $\frac{2}{32}$in on the treble. Then, with your radius gauge matched to the radius of the fretboard, get all the four remaining saddles meeting the gauge. Hopefully the additional angle and pitch of the neck will be enough and not too much; if it is not quite right, then the process will need to be done again with more or less of a shim.

Micro tilt system

Back in the 1970s Fender introduced the Micro-Tilt system on their guitars, at the time often with a three-screw neck plate. This simple leverage system had a small hole in the neck plate that allowed access to a metal disc that, when turned, would push up against the underside of the neck itself. With the neck screws loosened a little, the micro-tilt adjustment would increase the neck pitch, raising the neck angle. The adjustment would have the same result as fitting a shim inside the neck pocket. Afterwards, it was necessary to adjust the saddles, raising them due to the reduction in action height, and to get the action correct for the setup.

It also gives a better lead out of the saddle, and a pronounced angle to give a better attack directly over the bridge.

A shim can be created from 0.3mm (0.118in) or 0.5mm (0.157in) maple veneer, about 10mm deep and the width of the neck pocket. It is placed over the two holes nearest the neck pickup in the neck pocket. It does not need to be glued in – usually it is possible simply to let the neck screws go through the shim when tightening back up. As soon as the guitar is back to pitch it will be very noticeable that the action height has come down

CHAPTER 4

Bridge Saddle Radius

Understanding radius

After following the correct order of assessment and adjustment, and sorting out the neck relief and action height, you will need to look at the saddle radius. This is all about how the string height is proportional to the fretboard radius. The radius is the top of a curve of a specific length – if you pinned one end of a 9.5in piece of string to the bench, the top of that curve

would represent a 9.5in radius. A radius of 7.25in would be less and therefore more curved, and a radius of 12in would be the opposite; on a fretboard, this measurement makes quite a difference.

On a fixed-bridge guitar – most common in Gibson-style electrics – the radius of the fretboard is usually fairly shallow, at 12in or 16in, and the saddles within the bridge match the radius of the fretboard, usually with the two outer Es a little lower than the A and B string saddles

Radius of 16in.

and the D and G string saddles the highest. On some ABR-style bridges, the radius can be from the notch in the saddles, which are deeper on the outer strings and less deep towards the central two strings. The radius of these bridge saddles and therefore individual height are not adjustable; it is simply a case of setting the action height of the two outer E strings, and the other strings are set.

On the individual-saddled bridges that feature on almost all models of Fender-made guitars and their derivatives,

A radius of 7.25in.

OPPOSITE: 1963 Fender Stratocaster, recently set up and prepared for sale.

7.25"
There is a gap
in the middle
of the
fretboard

Fender
fretboard
radius of
7.25in.

9.5"
There is no gap
in the middle
of the
fretboard

Fender radius
of 9.5in.

12"
There is a gap
both sides of
the fretboard

Fender radius of 12in.

the saddles are adjustable. This is usually done with two grub screws per saddle that can be raised or lowered to get all the strings meeting the radius of the fretboard, giving a proportional string height across the fretboard.

The radius of the fretboard is very important for the feel and playability of a guitar. An instrument with a flatter radius can be slightly easier to play, certainly in terms of big bends and some chord positions. The natural shape of the player's finger is probably about 7.25 to 9.5in and when Leo Fender was inventing his guitars back in the 1950s the style of play that was current at the time may have influenced the shape of the fretboard. Bar chord playing is easier with a rounder fretboard, so the bridge on the guitar needed to be able to mirror that radius of the board. As Leo Fender was not a player himself, he is believed to have taken input from many guitarists and this could be why the fretboards had more radius. Indeed, his competition-made fretboards had a radius of 16in on average at the time.

When the saddles are under-radiused – in other words, flatter than the fretboard – there is a high likelihood that the strings will 'choke out' with a string bend, limiting the playability. When assessing this type of guitar and bridge setup, it is advisable to try out some tone and tone-and-a-half step bends to get a feel for the radius and how the strings play out while bending, as this takes the string up the curvature of the board.

It is more common for saddles to be slightly under-radiused on 7.25in radius boards, partly because it does look quite staggered, and partly because the grub screws on each saddle can vibrate and loosen, allowing the saddle to lower. It is an area that can be overlooked but it is as relevant as all the other setup points. When it is done well, there will often be a very positive reaction from the player. After teaching guitar setup for many years, it seems to me that the saddle radius is something that many players understand but rarely adjust, on the assumption that it is set and does not merit checking or changing. Also, they may not appreciate how much better the guitar can feel when the saddle radius matches the fretboard radius exactly.

Another knock-on effect of the saddles being under-radiused can be minor intonation flaws being picked up more acutely. If the board is 9.5in radius and the saddles are more like a 12in radius, for example, barring a chord will cause the middle strings to touch the fret first and with more pressure than the others. This means having to arc over the board more to get the outer Es and A and B better fretted, causing the D and G to lead off slightly sharp, as they have more pressure on them.

Under-radiused saddles can also affect the float of a bridge. The lower the saddles are in the middle of the bridge, the less tension there is over the bridge, which in turn means less lift. This effect is another typical setup point that is easily overlooked by the customer. The lack of float becomes the area of concern, and the owner looks at sorting out this part of the setup when it is actually the lack of radius that is the issue. The problem is often caused by inadequate maintenance, and a failure to keep the grub screws and saddles matching the fretboard radius.

Checking the radius

If you are unsure of the radius of a particular fretboard, you can take the opportunity during a re-stringing of the guitar to check it with a radius gauge. These are usually available in pairs for vintage boards, starting at 7.25in and going all the way up to 20in for flatter boards. They are usually inexpensive and another key tool for getting the best setup out of a range of guitars. It is possible to assess the radius

of a fretboard with the strings on the guitar, with the gauge placed over the top, but it is less accurate than when the strings are off.

It is always a good idea to check the fretboard radius at the 12th fret as well as at the 17th fret. The radius will usually be the same, but, if it is different, it will be flatter at the 17th. In this case, the fretboard radius is compound, often starting at 9.5in and going up to 16in. A compound radius

fretboard makes for comfortable playing of both open chords and bar chords, and for easy lead playing higher up the fretboard. With the fretboard getting flatter, the bends are easier and less likely to 'choke'. Most players go out of their way to get a compound board, so it probably will not be an accident if a guitar has this type of radius. When setting up a compound radius, getting the saddle radius to

Adjusting the saddle radius.

match the fretboard at the 12th or 17th fret is subject to the player's style. If they are more of a lead player, they will benefit from having a higher radius of the saddles/ strings – 16in is often the right radius for clean string bending and lead playing. If the player is more over the entire board, meeting the radius at the 12th fret might work well; it is subtle but worth playing with on a compound radius.

Adjusting the saddle radius

With the individual-saddled bridge and the neck relief correct or as desired, and the action heights measured at the 12th fret accurate or as desired, it is time to radius the strings matching the fretboard radius. With the guitar neck sitting on your left shoulder and the radius gauge

The guitar can be rested on the shoulder to adjust the radius.

placed lightly on the outer E strings, pluck each string. If they touch the radius gauge and rattle off the underside of it, this means they are radiused correctly. If they ring out, this indicates that they are under-radiused – sometimes this will be the case for all four of the middle strings. The outer Es are likely to be where they should be at this point.

To resolve any under-radius, take a small Allen key and raise each grub screw (on a six-saddle bridge) the same amount, enabling the saddle to increase in height parallel to the bridge plate, until the string vibrates and buzzes off the underside of the radius gauge. When all the strings are touching the underside of the radius gauge, they are radiused correctly. With any adjustment the strings will go sharp or flat; more commonly, they will go sharp, as the bridge saddles are often under-radiused before adjustment. Because of this, it is vital always to keep an eye on the tuning, especially with a floating bridge. Any raising of the saddles may also put some tension in the neck, and definitely in the float of the bridge. Keeping on top of the tuning after each adjustment will help with any such issues.

Case study: Fender Telecaster

With all the measurements assessed, this Fender Telecaster appears to be well set up. The neck relief and action heights are both fine, but the guitar 'chokes out' when bending one of the high unwound strings. Checking the radius by placing the gauge on the outer E strings indicates that the

middle four strings are too low to meet the fretboard radius. This is the reason for the choking. When the string is bent, its angle to the bridge becomes too shallow and the note drops off and chokes. Not ideal during a solo!

With the guitar neck leaning on the shoulder, the gauge is placed just over the bridge pickup (the pull of the magnet steadies the gauge a little, without pulling the gauge in), and each string is gently plucked in turn. In this position, it is possible not only to see but also to hear whether the central strings are low. If the string resonates, that indicates a lower radius to the saddles. The saddles can be raised by turning the grub screws and the string is then plucked again and observed, to see whether the saddle is meeting the radius. This is done with all four central strings and then the guitar is re-tuned to pitch and tested in that troublesome high-register area for big bends. The result should be a significant reduction in choking. In the case of this Fender Telecaster, this turned out to be the only part of the current setup that was impeding the guitar's playability.

When adjusting the saddle radius, especially on a floating-bridge guitar, it is important to be aware of the potential knock-on effect. As always, it is vital to have a record of how the guitar was when you started work on it, and to follow the proper order of the setup. Any change in saddle radius will affect the floating of the bridge. If the strings are raised, there will be more tension over them, and this will increase the float of the bridge. It is not uncommon to start off with very little float in the bridge and to find that getting the radius correct gives the correct float.

CHAPTER 5

Floating the Bridge

Floating bridges and the tremolo system

A bridge is said to be 'floating' when it is not fixed down to the body with mounting studs and/or a tailpiece and 'floats' on top of the body. This allows the strings to be flattened or sharpened with the use of a tremolo arm. Usually, a floating bridge is held in with either six screws at the front of the bridge or a claw and springs in a cavity in the back of the guitar. The bridge claw springs hold the bridge back whilst the tension in the strings pulls it forward; when these two tensions meet, the bridge is then floating, in a balancing act between springs and strings. All floating bridges are involved in this balancing act, whether they have six or two screw fixings or have a cavity behind the bridge for the bridge to be pulled back very sharply, as is the case on a Floyd Rose bridge, a type that is often found on Ibanez guitars, ESP, and so on.

The tremolo system has been around since the 1930s, but it was not until Paul Bigsby came up with a version that greatly improved tuning stability that this great bit of hardware was here to stay. Leo Fender's synchronised tremolo unit was first

OPPOSITE: PRS Custom24, serviced and set up.

introduced in 1954 on the Stratocaster, using a trem block fitted through a cavity in the body, connecting to (usually) three springs attached to the claw in the rear of the guitar. With six individual saddles, the change in pitch when lowering or pulling back created 'synchronised' pitch bend to the strings. The routing for the block and

cavity for the claw and the use of springs create a natural reverberation chamber, so the bridge and its setup are all part of the tone too.

With any tremolo system, the aim is not only to create some nice vibrato but also to return to pitch, and not flat or sharp. This is where a good tech or a good setup will

Floating bridge with a lot of lift.

Floating bridge with a low amount of lift.

Maximum amount of lift ⁴⁄₃₂in.

Measuring the lift of the bridge ²⁄₃₂in.

the front of the bridge, enabling the bridge to rest back in position. Sometimes, one or two will be touching the bridge plate or sitting at a slight angle, which will cause a jerky action on the trem arm.

If you find that the bridge does have a jerky movement when you are about to re-set the float, unscrew the middle four mounting screws and test the movement of the bridge with the trem arm. If it is smooth, then re-insert each screw and re-test after fitting each one. You may discover that one hole is slightly out of line, often by the finest of margins. You can either fill and dowel the hole if you are set up for repairs. If you do not have the facilities or tools for this, try turning the screw anti-clockwise to raise it ever so slightly and prevent the angle causing any friction. A very delicate turn may be all that is required.

Measuring the lift on a bridge

really help. In common with all the previous setup steps, there are many factors that may have a direct knock-on effect on the function of the floating bridge. The general maintenance of the guitar will also have an impact on tuning stability.

With a 'vintage'-style tremolo bridge, of the type found on many a Fender Strat, as well as Squiers, vintage and all the other copies of this style, there are six mounting screws. These play a vital role in keeping the movement of the floating bridge in good shape – the less friction on the screws, the better. To achieve the smoothest action, all six screws need to be well fitted and not putting any pressure on

Fender's factory specs state that the float of the bridge, also known as the lift, is between ⅓₂in and ⁴⁄₃₂in measured at the back and underside of the bridge to the top of the body. The amount of lift determines how much the player can pull back on the tremolo arm and sharpen the strings, perhaps to meet a specific note. For example, pulling back and meeting the body may cause the notes to sharpen by a semi-tone; this would be a relatively small amount of lift. For an increase of a full tone, the bridge would require more lift of approximately ²⁄₃₂in, or more.

The amount of lift required can be a subjective topic and most players, customers and techs probably do not have a particular measurement in mind. It is more common to set the lift by eye; understanding the manufacturers' parameters for lift is a good place to start. For players who require only a little palm vibrato and do not use the tremolo arm, a lift of ⅓₂in will probably be suitable. For players who do use the tremolo arm, the lift would have to be more, from ²⁄₃₂in to ³⁄₃₂in. For full use of the bridge, the highest amount of lift – ⁴⁄₃₂in – would be required.

The best way to find out how the bridge needs to be set on this style of guitar is to go back to the player's style and consider their use or otherwise of the tremolo. Many players simply want the bridge flat to the body, so that the tuning stability is solid, but this is based on an assumption that any float will mean that the strings will not hold tune. However, if the float of the bridge is well set up, and all the other setup and maintenance points are at an optimum and covered, the tuning will be fine. Indeed, it will be greatly improved with the addition of some decent new strings – dirt on the strings can easily make its way down the string to the nut, causing the string to bind in the nut. This can lead to tuning issues, especially when putting some vibrato into the string, as the string's ease of movement through the nut is hindered.

The balancing act

For the bridge and strings to return to pitch there needs to be a good balance between the strings and the springs. Where string and spring tension meet, the bridge will always return to its position before flattening or sharpening. The gauge of string and the number of springs, as well as the position of the claw in the cavity in the back of the guitar, all play an important role whilst considering the player's style and usage of the trem. As a rough guide, for a set of 8s or 9s (0.008in/0.009in–0.040in/0.042in) two or three springs would usually be enough to balance string and spring tension. For 10s (0.010–0.046in), it is most common to have three springs; for any higher gauge, there will be four or five springs.

The lift can be at any angle with either two, three or five springs; it all depends on how much the claw is tightened or loosened.

To increase or reduce the amount of lift on a vintage Stratocaster-style tremolo, it is necessary first to take the tension out of the strings and allow the bridge to rest flat on the body. This way, there is no tension held in either and the adjustment is easier. In the past, and always with my first Squier Strat, I tried to change the lift whilst at full tension. Tightening the claw screws in order to reduce the amount of lift was pretty tough and did not seem to achieve a great deal visually or when measured. In fact, the result was that the strings had

Adjusting the claw screws.

gone sharp, meaning that the bridge had pulled in a little and possibly reduced in height.

The first thing to do after changing the lift is to re-tune the guitar, starting at the Bass E, which needs flattening off to get back to pitch. This results in the tension being reduced on the bridge and the rest of the strings sharpening a little without you noticing. The A string now needs flattening and the D string is almost showing an E on the tuner! By the time you get that to pitch, the bridge is pretty much flat to the body and no longer has any lift at all. It only takes a small half-turn on the claw screws to make a noticeable difference; when done at pitch, this can cause unnecessary issues. When the strings are slackened off and the bridge rests, it is easier to tighten or loosen the claw screws and then, when slowly bringing the tuning back up to pitch, going from Bass E to Treble E, the bridge will come to rest when the string and spring tension is met. The tuning will move around while you bring it back to pitch so that, even though you start off with the Bass E correct, by the time the rest of the strings are correct, the Bass E will have gone flat. This is a result of the bridge pulling up under the tension of the other strings. Only when you get back to the Bass E and that is stable can you measure the float of the bridge and see where it has ended up. At that point, you have met string and spring tension.

If you find that some of the strings have gone sharp, it is a good idea to slacken them off and then bring them back to pitch slowly, starting with the Bass E and moving to the Treble E. In this case, the springs are winning and that can be much harder to settle.

Case study: adjusting the float of a Fender Strat bridge

This Fender Stratocaster, fitted with the vintage six screws, had 10s on it and three springs in the back. When the guitar came in there was no lift on the bridge and the owner wanted to use the tremolo arm for some nice vibrato. They were not aiming for any huge dive bombs, which would not have been practical on this guitar anyway, but for some nice shimmers and movement. All the setup points were checked beforehand and, as all were spot on, it was suggested that the lack of lift on the bridge might be due to the claw springs being tightened at some point, to hold the bridge tight to the body. The six screws looked to be sitting well and, when pressing down on the tremolo arm, the movement of the bridge felt smooth and frictionless. Clearly, it was time to go in and sort out the claw screws.

First, the string was slackened off a few tones. (Top tip: count the number of winds down that you do on each machine head and make sure that they are even. This way, when you take it back to pitch, you can simply count back up. This will get you closer to the correct pitch and should help you get the strings settled at pitch. The same applies with a vintage-style truss rod adjustment.) With the guitar on the bench face down and with the back plate removed, the bridge claw was unscrewed and by a full turn. (These are large screws that hold a great deal of spring and string pressure, so they require much more significant amounts of adjustment than, for example, the truss rods.) Experience has shown that, for about a ⅓₂in lift gain on the bridge, a full turn is needed. Springs are all different in terms of length and strength, but going in either a half-turn or full turn of the claw screws should not result in too much change.

With the guitar back on the bench the right way round, it was slowly brought back to pitch (counting up initially) and then going through from Bass E to Treble E until the strings and springs settled, and a balanced tension was maintained. The bridge lift was then measured, at just over ⅓₂in. This amount was good for some gentle vibrato but not for pulling back with more attack, which would mean that the bridge would knock on the top of the body. Another adjustment was needed.

The strings were again slackened off an even amount and then another full turn was made on the claw screws and the guitar re-tuned slowly, working from Bass E to Treble E. Once the tuning had settled, the result of the adjustment was ⅔₂in lift at the

Alternative floating bridges for Bigsby's tremolo system.

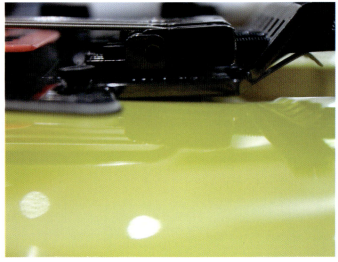

Floyd Rose bridge with too much lift.

Floyd Rose bridge with too little lift.

Floyd Rose bridge set at 'Zero'.

back of the bridge. This amount of lift with this gauge of string meant a nice amount of pull back without knocking the top of the body, unless the player was really aggressive. Palm vibrato was still easy and the tuning stable. Sometimes, perhaps when there has been more of a change using the tremolo, working the strings and springs will help settle the bridge even more. It may pull up the slightest bit or on occasion pull back, but the tuning of the guitar will indicate this, as it goes flat or sharp. Most of the time, and especially when patiently following the tuning back up from Bass E to Treble E, the bridge will rest and settle.

The Floyd Rose bridge

The balancing act between strings and springs is the same in theory with all styles of floating trem. The American Standard has two mounting screws, while the PRS version has six screws or two mounting studs, which need to be flush to the bridge. Holding it at 'Zero', simply raising or lowering these and then working on the claw will allow you to get the lift height right. Floyd Rose bridges are the same again, although the body usually has a cavity behind the

bridge so when set at 'Zero' the bridge can be pulled quite far back, making the strings very sharp. The difference with the Floyd Rose system is that the strings are locked in with a locking nut. The idea behind this is that, once the bridge is set correctly, the strings can be locked in so when you flatten or sharpen the strings they will return to their earlier position at pitch. This definitely works, but it does still require a good set of well-stretched strings. Any major stretching of the strings can result in them going slightly flat, no matter how much they are engineered not to.

CHAPTER 6

Intonation

Understanding intonation and scale length

Intonation is all about string length compensation. Every guitar has a scale length, which is the distance between the leading edge of the nut and the intonation line where the bridge is placed. Each bridge has adjustable saddles that can be moved behind or forward of this line, compensating the accuracy of the intonation.

A fretted instrument is an imperfect instrument and will only play in tune up to a point. An E on the keyboard of a piano will always be an E; if it is played hard, it will be a loud E, but it will still be an E. On the other hand, when a guitar player plucks or strums Bass E as hard as they can it will almost be an F, will eventually get to E and then fall flat as it decays. As a result, it is possible to be accurate about the guitar's intonation only in relation to the mathematics of the scale length and fret position.

Intonation must be the final process in the setup as all the other points – neck relief, action, radiusing and even the float of the bridge – will make a difference. The other point with intonating is to test and adjust in the playing position, which is how you or a customer will be hearing it. There will be a difference in intonation between a guitar with a floating bridge or maybe a super heavy Gibson Les Paul on its back on the bench or behind the player's head. Using a Peterson Strobe tuner, which is very accurate and sensitive, it is quite easy to see that when a Strat is turned upside down, the tuning is out.

Another factor that can affect the intonation and accuracy is the condition of the strings. If they are very dirty, the readings can differ compared with a fresh set. Most of the time, it is possible to carry out all the other setup points prior to this point with the slightly old strings, followed by all the maintenance points, then re-string and stretch in the new strings. Intonating is then the very last thing to be done on the guitar. Most of the time a fresh set of strings is not needed but it is good practice to finalise the intonation with the current strings and then, once the new set are on, after the maintenance points, double-check the intonation in the playing position.

Scale length will define fret position. A mathematical rule of 17.817 gives the

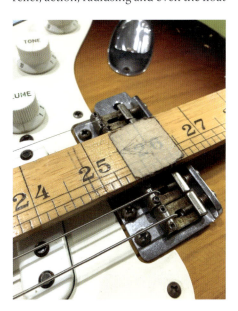

Fender with a scale length of 25.5in.

Fender with a scale length of 25.5in at the bridge.

OPPOSITE: Gibson L5, one of the nicest electric jazz guitars, serviced and set up.

nut to 1st fret distance and all the way up the fretboard. So, with a 24.75in scale, the distance between the frets is slightly less than on a longer scale of 25.5in.

For every cent (1/100th of a semitone) of a note, the string length compensation is 0.010in. Although it is not necessary to work out exactly how sharp or flat a note is, the maths can be proven on a tuner that indicates cents of a note, such as the Peterson Strobe tuner. Although some customers do have their tuning ear really dialled in, most people cannot discern whether a note is sharp or flat by less than 3 cents of a note. If you are hearing that a note is sharp or flat, it is more than likely by more than 3 cents and probably more than 5 cents, meaning that the saddle has to move at

least 0.030–0.050in, which is a noticeable change.

Scale length will also change the tone of the guitar to some extent. A short scale of, say, 24.75in, such as that mainly used on Gibson guitars and their derivatives, tends to give a warmer tone. It enables the strings to be bent a little more easily, as they have less tension over them than is the case with a long scale of 25.5in, with strings of the same gauge. The long scale produces a brighter, more articulate sound, which is why a Strat's tone is often described as 'bell-like'. Big bends are still possible, but the strings have a little more tension.

This consideration for scale length and intonation can lead to a need for string gauge changes, so that two guitars of

differing scale lengths can feel the same for a guitarist. A guitar of 24.75in scale length could have a set of 11-gauge strings and the Strat a set of 10-gauge strings, and the feel in the strings of both would be very similar.

The condition of the frets plays an important role in how well intonated a guitar can be and understanding the scale length and fret positioning highlights this. The fret has a barbed part called the tang, which sits in the fret slot. It is calculated according to scale length, so the tang is the exact centre point of the fret. Frets that are worn as a result of playing, with indents or flat spots, will not intonate as well as they should due to the leading edge not being perfectly in the centre and on top of a well-crowned fret. When a guitar is on the bench for setting up, the issue of fret

Gibson with a scale length of 24.75in.

Gibson with a scale length of 24.75in at the bridge.

wear can be most noticeable when a tech is trying to intonate. Well-dressed frets will intonate much better than worn ones. According to the mathematical rule of 1 cent equals 0.010in, a fret that is 0.100in wide intonates at 0.050in. If that fret is very worn and flattened off from years of play, then the leading edge, or the spot where that note is fretting, could be up to 0.050in away from the centre of the fret. It would therefore be 5 cents sharp or flat, which would be very noticeable, and this could occur anywhere on the fretboard.

The cut of the nut will also influence the intonation, and this will be more noticeable over the open-chord positions. If the cut of the nut and its leading edge are not at a good angle and the string does not lead off the leading edge (fretboard edge), then the scale length can be extended slightly, making a note sharp over the nut. Sometimes, it can be the nut height that is the issue too.

A guitar may well need additional work in order to get the best out of it. In general, if the desired setup is being compromised and intonation is one area that may become problematic, then a fret dress should be considered. For information on fret dressing, levelling and re-crowning, *see* Chapter 17.

Adjustment for intonation: Gibson, Fender, Gretsch, Epiphone, Ibanez and others

When all other setup points have been done and you are ready to intonate, hold the guitar comfortably in your lap in the playing position, either with the existing strings (if they are still in good shape) or

with a fresh set of strings that have been stretched in (*see* Chapter 11). Re-tune or double-check the tuning. For a floating bridge-style guitar, it is definitely worth checking all the strings. One string being a semi-tone or a tone down will affect the lift on the bridge and possibly the overall tension in the guitar, and this might throw the intonation out very slightly when all is at pitch. Always double-check the tuning.

Gibson ABR intonation adjustment.

Play the open string with a medium level of attack – not too soft and not too heavy – so the note is not flat or going sharp on the attack, then fret the 12th fret with the same level of attack in the centre on the fret. Do this without bending the string either behind the fret a little or into the fretboard, as this will make the note sharper. The open E and the fretted note at the 12th fret should be the same because

Fender Jazzmaster intonation adjustment.

points at their optimum and/or suited to the player's style, the best you can do as a tech is to be consistent with the level of attack when you are making adjustments for intonation. The rest is up to the player! Quite often, when you have set up a guitar for someone else, being as sensitive as possible to the intonation, it will be played with a heavy attack and notes being bent whilst chording, and this will highlight interval inaccuracies. It is not possible to take into account how hard a player might fret a note anywhere on the fretboard, so approaching the adjustment with a medium level of attack open and fretted attack – as well as being sure of all the setup numbers – is the best one can do (without getting into compensating the nut and pitch offsetting).

Proving the maths

To use the 1 cent equals 0.010in in scale length compensation, you can precisely measure how many cents of a note the fretted note is sharp or flat. That measurement can then be put on the dial calipers and carefully transferred to the saddle. Taking this measurement requires a tuner that holds cents of a note. Peterson Strobe is the industry standard brand for this and the Strobo pedal tuner is one of the best in the price range. Someone who is planning on setting up guitars professionally, including acoustics, would be well advised to invest in the best tuner they can afford.

In this example, the guitar was held in the playing position, and the tuner set to manual on the G string, open note to fretted. It established that the note was 7 cents sharp, which meant that the scale needed to be lengthened by 0.070in. This

the 12th fret is the mid-way point in the scale and the octave.

If the fretted 12th note is sharp, you will need to extend the scale by moving the saddle back in the bridge. If the note is flat, then the scale from the leading edge of the nut to the true intonation line will need to be shortened.

Remember:

- Sharp = Lengthen the scale. Screw the saddle back.
- Flat = Shorten the scale. Unscrew the saddle to move it forward.

The adjustment can be done in the playing position, usually with a flat-head screwdriver for most ABR and Nashville-style bridges or with a Phillips head for most floating-bridge and individual-saddled guitars. There is no specified number of turns to be made, but the saddle does need to be seen to move if the tuner is showing that the fretted note is either sharp or flat.

With any adjustment, the note will go sharp if you are lengthening the scale or flat if shortening, so after every adjustment the tuning on that string needs to be re-tuned and back up to pitch. It is always best to bring the note up to pitch rather than down to pitch, as the string is more settled that way. Once back at the correct pitch, play the open string as accurately as you can and then the fretted note at the 12th fret again. Hopefully, the notes will be the same. Pay attention to how the note falls flat or holds on the tuner. The more accurate you can be, and the more equal the open note and the fretted note fall flat, the better the intonation.

This needs to be done for each string.

Having an accurate tuner and being consistent and careful with your tuning will help you achieve the best intonation. It also helps to be aware of the open string attack as well as the fretted, and to try to get an equal temperament between the two notes. Essentially, with all setup

Adjusting the intonation in the playing position.

Double-checking the intonation in the playing position.

The Peterson Strobe tuner is highly accurate and capable of holding cents of a note.

and the fretted at the 12th played. Both were exactly the same.

Intonating in this way is beyond what is usually needed for the general setting up of your own guitars, or those of others. It is very rare that electric guitars on the bench have needed this practical application, but it could become useful when all the saddles and their intonation seem to be a similar amount out. If you are able to measure how much each note is out, you can then move the saddles back or forth by that amount, and get closer to the correct position. You can then fine-tune the intonation after that.

Compensated tuning systems

is done by screwing the saddle back by that amount. Carefully holding the dial calipers over the saddle with the edge nut side at its leading edge, the screws were tightened to move the saddle back until it was at the bridge side of the calipers (0.070in). The guitar was then re-tuned, the tuner re-set to G, and the open note While I was studying guitar building and repair in 2007, the Buzz Feiten tuning system (BFTS) was only a couple of years old, but it was proving to be a very accurate way to solve intonation issues. Buzz Feiten was a high-profile session player who, having been accused by a pianist of being out of tune, double-checked his tuning to discover that he was actually at the correct pitch across all strings. The experience did, however, highlight tuning issues over certain chord positions and keys.

Feiten's aim in creating BFTS was to solve tuning and intonation flaws. He did it by introducing a shelf nut, which cuts down the distance from the leading edge of the nut to the first fret. This reduces how sharp the first few frets are, around the open-chord positions. The shelf nut is made with precision, based on scale length, fret width and string gauge. Once the nut has been made, the guitar is intonated using patented pitch offsets, resulting in an even and balanced intonation across the fretboard.

The system definitely works. As a qualified retro fitter of the system for both electric and acoustic guitars, I have 'Feitenised' many instruments. To my mind (and ear), it makes the notes across the entire fretboard sit up straight. It does take a bit of getting used to and players often comment that they need to relearn how to play certain chords. Guitarists are always compensating a little, perhaps without realising. With 'perfect' intonation, the player needs to play it perfectly, otherwise the gain is minimalised. Another factor that determines the outcome of the system is how good the frets are on the board. If they are worn, the intonation can be compromised. This is something that can affect any fretboard and setup, but in this case it can be the reason why the guitar will not intonate to the accurate pitch offsets. The best solution may be a fret dress, but not all guitar owners are keen on spending a few hundred pounds getting everything done.

Earvana is another compensated tuning system that also has a shelf nut. This is staggered according to three rules: pitch, tension and mass. Like the BFTS, its aim is to achieve equal temperament in the notes. The Earvana nut costs a lot less than the BFTS version and may be a bit more accessible, but replacing the nut for a shelf nut does need to include a full setup. Replacing an existing nut in a guitar with an Earvana may seem relatively straightforward, but it can often prove tricky. Nuts are sometimes glued in a little too much and do not come out cleanly, so the change will require the expertise and tools of a tech.

Generally, if all the setup points on a guitar are very accurate, it has good new strings, and the cut of the nut is right, then the natural intonation flaws inherent in a fretted instrument will be kept to a minimum. It is so often the case that any intonation issues can be traced to another setup point being incorrect. Once this setting has been sorted out, the intonation will usually fall within the tolerance of 3 cents of a note.

Once all the setup points have been correctly measured and adjusted, the regular maintenance of the guitar can start. (If the strings are past their prime, the six maintenance points are the starting point.) Again, the order of the various steps of maintenance is important, but in this case it is more for efficiency.

PART TWO

Guitar Maintenance

CHAPTER 7

Fretboards

A range of materials is used for making the fretboards on electric guitars, from the more common and traditional – maple, rosewood and ebony – to newer variants, such as pau ferro, padauk, ovangkol, and more exotic woods such as cocobolo and ziricote. There are also synthetic woods such as Richlite and Micarta. The material plays a role in the tone and the feel of the instrument in the hands of the player and maintenance of the fretboard is very important in terms of that feel and playability when it comes to setup.

With some hours of play, the fretboard can build up layers of dirt and grime. On the darker woods this can be slightly less noticeable but upon closer inspection it can be easily seen piling up between the frets. On a maple fretboard, for example, it will be more obvious. Regular cleaning will prevent this build-up and make the fretboard and playing area so much nicer to use.

Cleaning an unfinished fretboard

Unfinished boards, such as those made from rosewood and ebony, can be cleaned

with ultra-fine 0000 furniture-grade wire wool. The wire wool that is more readily available at DIY/hardware stores – usually 000-grade – is too rough; in my experience, it can almost pull the frets out.

Using 0000-grade wool with some wood oil soap will gently lift the dirt and debris from the fretboard. Once the fretboard has been cleaned, it may need some conditioner. Lemon oil is commonly used –

0000-grade wire wool.

sometimes far too liberally – but care must be taken, as oil above 2% purity can be damaging to the guitar. If the frets are glued, the oil can erode this over time as well as the glue on the bindings. There are wood oil soaps that can be used to clean the fretboard and condition the wood at the same time; these are great for any unfinished fretboard.

On unfinished boards, the frets will also benefit from cleaning with 0000-grade wire wool, appearing brighter and more polished.

When a rosewood fretboard has been caked in grime for years, a good clean with oil soap and 0000-grade wire wool can result in it looking a little dull, or even rather grey. This is because all those lovely nutrients from the player's dirt and sweat have been removed! It can be resolved with the application of some good-quality beeswax with turpentine. This is very easy to apply with a finger and, once the entire board has been covered, it can be wiped off with some workshop towel. This will make the fretboard appear well nourished and feel good to touch. There are many different waxes with combinations of natural products on the market today, and each tech will have their own preference, as will many guitarists.

Wood oil soap is good for gently cleaning the fretboard.

Using 0000-grade wire wool and wood oil soap on unfinished fretboards.

Cleaning the fretboard, following the grain up and down the neck.

Cleaning up with a fresh towel after using wire wool and oil soap.

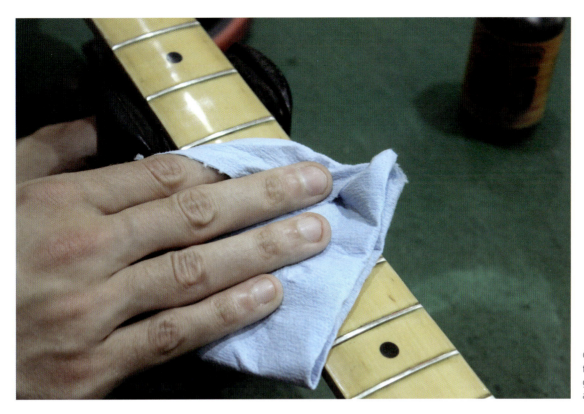

Cleaning a finished fretboard with a good pump polish and a cloth.

Cleaning a finished fretboard

On a finished fretboard, such as those made from maple on a Fender-style guitar, the wood will have been lacquered in the same way as the neck in either a vintage gloss, clear gloss or satin finish. This type of fretboard can be cleaned using a good-quality guitar pump polish such as Dunlop 65, Gibson pump polish or any of the other branded guitar cleaners, applied with a rag or some fine towel and then polished off. Dunlop 65 is one of the best as it is quite fine and does not take very long to clean off.

If a finished fretboard is very dirty, applying some of the cleaner directly to the board will help. With this type of fretboard, as the finish on the neck is usually the same (gloss and lacquered), the back of neck can also be cleaned at the same time.

Technique

With either type of fretboard, and with the strings off, the board should be cleaned from the 21st/22nd fret up to the nut and back down, following the grain rather than going across the fretboard, and slowly working with the radius of the fretboard. Some areas, particularly around the open-chord positions, may need some more attention than others.

When using 0000-grade wire wool on a guitar that has either a humbucker-style or single-coil setup, it is wise to avoid getting too close to the neck pickup. A couple of pieces of masking tape placed gently over the pickup should protect it from any metal filings. If any debris does get on to the pickup, it can be easily removed with a paintbrush.

It takes very little time to make the fretboard look and feel great again so, rather than allowing the build-up of a lot of dirt, it is highly recommended to clean it with every string change.

CHAPTER 8

Fret Polishing

Without regular maintenance the frets will tarnish, making them appear very dull, and sometimes even a little green. They can also start to feel rough. Frets in this condition are not great to play on, do not feel very quick or easy and certainly look pretty bad. Some guitar players and owners seem to cause the frets to tarnish more quickly than others – this can be down to how they sweat and even their type of sweat. Guitars that are left on hangers in a room can slowly tarnish without play, while those that are used by players who do not venture up the fretboard (the dusty end!) very often will also tarnish worse there than in the playing positions.

The frets on unfinished boards will clean up well with the use of wire wool and a wood oil soap/conditioner on the board, and may look as though they do not need any polishing up afterwards. However, considering the short amount of time it takes, it is always worth giving them another rub. On a finished board, a pump polish and cloth will not always clean up the frets satisfactorily. Fret polishing on either an unfinished or finished fretboard is made much easier with the use of a fret guard. This handy tool sits

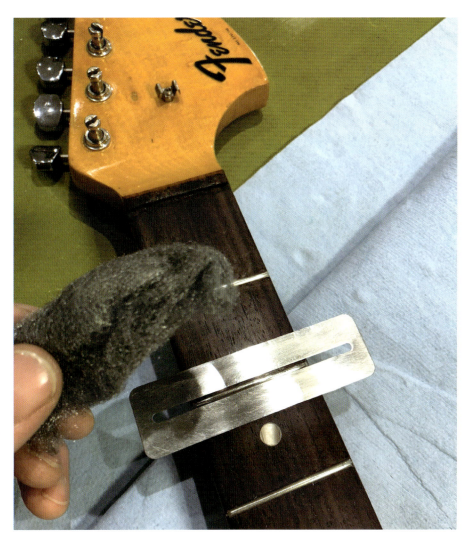

A fret guard can be used to protect the fretboard.

OPPOSITE: PRS McCarty 594 serviced and set up.

Fret guard and wire wool.

Polishing the frets on a maple board.

Polishing the higher register frets on a maple board can take a little more time.

Micromesh papers of 1500- to 12,000-grit.

Lovely polished-up frets.

Frets feel great to play polished.

on the fretboard and exposes the relevant fret, which can then be polished with wire wool of the same grade. Gently rubbing the fret from side to side, working from one side of the fret over to the other, will clean it up nicely, making it bright and shiny.

Another product that can be used to get frets looking great is micromesh papers, super-fine polishing papers that usually come as 3 × 3in pieces. They tend to start at 1500-grit and go up in 1000-grit increments to 12,000-grit.

Using the fret guard, each fret is gently rubbed and polished, working up through the grit increments. The 1500-grit paper actually feels quite coarse and will dull the fret slightly, but proceeding through the grades will make any score marks finer and finer, up to 12,000 grit, which will make the frets appear incredibly smooth and very polished. Micromesh papers are fairly expensive and using them takes a lot more time than using 0000-grade wire wool, with more or less the same end result. As long as

the frets are polished regularly with each string change, simply using wire wool will be a more cost-effective and time-saving way of getting frets that look and feel great.

Fret polishing is not done just for aesthetic reasons. It also improves the guitar's playability. Fresh new strings over the top of nicely polished frets feel superb to play on and make for a great finish to the setup. Shiny frets are often the first thing to be noticed by the uninitiated! If it is done regularly, the process takes no time at all.

CHAPTER 9

Electrics

Regular cleaning and maintenance of the volume and tone pots, as well as the switches, is important to keep any electric guitar playing well. Over time, dust and dirt can get between the slider inside a pot. As the volume or tone is turned down, the dirt may cause the contact to be missed slightly, resulting in some audible crackles. In the worst case, the sliders can rest on the dust and dirt and the volume and output will be cut. Semi-hollow-bodied guitars tend to be worse than the solid bodies due to the F hole, which allows more dust and debris inside the guitar and then into the pots.

On nearly all electric guitars, the pots and switches may be accessed by removing the scratch plate, control plate or back plate. On semi-hollow-bodied guitars and electric archtops, the pots are less accessible. The pots and the electrics can be cleaned, but the procedure is a little trickier.

On Fender Strats and all their variants, the pickups and controls are easy to clean as they are fixed to the scratch plate. Cleaning the pots when all the strings are off, during a routine string change, will keep any crackling to a minimum, or eliminate it completely. Removing all the screws and laying them out on the bench in the order and shape of the plate will help, especially when working on a vintage Strat, when getting the screws back in the same place might be key. You may find that the screws are more corroded in the playing positions. With the screws out you can lift the plate up, turn it through 90 degrees and place it inside the body cavity. There should be enough ground wire from the bridge claw, as well as enough wire from the jack socket, to

CTS pot cleaned out with the nozzle from a good contact cleaner.

OPPOSITE: Gibson Byrdland: a shorter-scale beauty that is always a pleasure to have in the workshop.

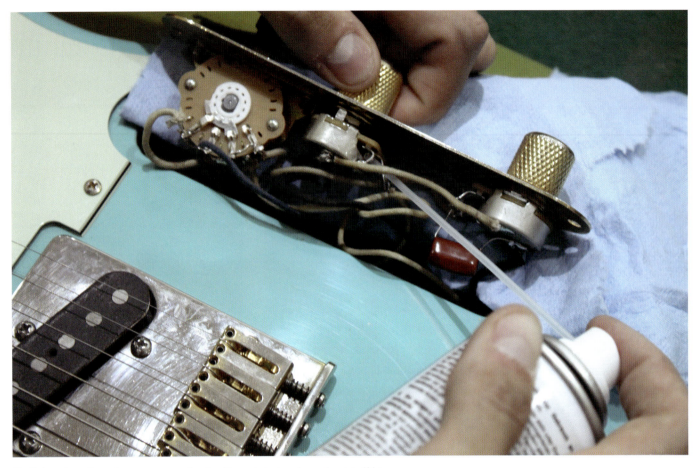

On Telecasters, there is easy access allowing the pots to be cleaned out swiftly.

Gibson pots are accessed and cleaned by removing the back plate.

By removing the scratch-plate screws, the pots on Strat-style guitars can be gently exposed and cleaned.

allow for this. Some cloth or workshop towel underneath the plate will protect the finish and pick up any overspray of the switch cleaner.

On Fender Telecasters and their variants, the volume, tone and switch controls are mounted to a control plate, which can easily be removed from the body by removing the two mounting screws. The plate is then carefully pulled up and flipped over to expose the electrics. The job is so easy, having crackly pots is inexcusable!

On most Gibsons, the electrics are accessible through a plate on the back of the guitar. This allows easy cleaning of the pots without the strings having to be off.

Semi-hollow-bodied guitars from Gibson and other manufacturers require

WD contact cleaner is an industry standard.

The 3-way or 5-way switches on Tele and Strat styles of guitar can sometimes be cleaned with contact cleaner, as can 3-way toggles. However, with both style of switch, any issues are usually related to the volume or tone pots. If you do want to use a contact cleaner, Servisol, Deoxit and WD Contact are all industry standards that have been used for years now. They always seem to clean out the pots very well and without any negative effect on any finishes. Even so, it is always a good idea to put some cloth or paper towel underneath to catch any overspray, just in case.

There have been many cases in the repair shop where there is no output at all on a guitar. Although it may seem to be a result of an issue with the electrics, output jack or pickups, it is always worth cleaning out the pots first. This was the case with a nice Epiphone Sheraton (semi-hollows are always the worst) that had no output at all, at any switch position, and anywhere on the volume and tone pots. The local shop had suggested that it needed new pickups. With the guitar on the bench and plugged in, the pots were thoroughly flushed out and continually turned from 0 to 10. After a thorough clean, the output returned, at every position on the 3-way, and both volumes and both tones worked perfectly well. The guitar did not need anything else doing, so the customer saved a load of money from not having to buy new pickups!

With regular cleaning, dirt, dust and debris will not build up in the pots, so this should be done with every setup. No matter how regularly the guitar is in and on the bench, checking for any output issues should definitely be a first port of call. It could save a lot of time and money.

more luck than judgement! Using a can of switch cleaner, you might be able to get the straw inside the F hole and clean out the volume pots pretty well. It is usually more difficult to do the tone pots, but it will be successful most of the time. A few lutherie suppliers sell a tube and cap that can fit over the top of the pot once the knob has been removed. This will send the contact cleaner down the shaft of the pot with a little more success than simply pointing and spraying. Schatten tools have a very good knob puller that is especially useful for this.

Potentiometers, switches and jacks can all get dust and dirt in them. This can tarnish them and cause crackling when they are used. Volume and tone pots will also often crackle when they have not been cleaned out. Doing it regularly during every string change should prevent any build-up of dirt. The volume or tone pot has a slider inside that makes contact and enables the signal either to go to ground or to bring more of the capacitor into the circuit. When dust finds its way in between the slider and its contact point, crackling can occur.

CHAPTER 10

General Cleaning

Different finishes

Most electric guitars are manufactured using one of a couple of methods and styles of finish; essentially, this is either poly-based (polyurethane, polyester) or 'nitro' (nitrocellulose or lacquer). Mass-produced guitars are often poly-based, while higher-end guitars usually have a nitro finish. This is because the latter is more costly and time-consuming to apply. Poly can be sprayed on thick and then cut back more easily, as it is a harder finish. Nitrocellulose paint, on the other hand, has to be layered up slowly and then sanded back at intervals until it has built up sufficiently and is flat. It is then buffed to a high shine. Poly is much more durable but, when damaged, it does chip quite badly. Nitro will age less well, as it is always off-gassing, but the effects of this ageing may add to the tone of the guitar and result in a pleasing appearance. Vintage instruments that look and sound great may do so because the finish has slowly become thinner and thinner, allowing the wood to have a particular tonal character.

If you are unsure what finish a guitar has, the manufacturer's websites usually provide adequate information about the finishes that they use. As a guide, poly feels a little thick and slightly plasticky, while nitro usually has a slightly sweet smell. Developed for the car industry, nitrocellulose spray-on paint was used extensively in the 1950s and 1960s, when it was adopted by guitar manufacturers as the finish to use. Many stunning guitars were finished during those decades with nitro colours that had been designed for painting cars, including Fiesta Red, Daphne Blue and Cadillac Green. Some would change colour over the years, creating new variants in modern times, but the origins lay in the car industry.

When working on a vintage instrument, it is reasonable to assume that it was finished with nitro paint. In this case, more care will be needed, especially if the finish has 'checked' – that is to say, it is showing the fine lines and cracking that tend to occur over time due to minor expansions and contractions. There may be crazing all over the body and neck, and on the headstock too.

This appearance is what many modern 'aged' and 'relic' guitars are aiming for.

Cleaning methods and products

Regardless of whether the guitar has a nitro- or poly-based finish, the body and neck may be cleaned using one of the pump polishes that are available from the main manufacturers. Most are good and will not harm the finish. Fender's Custom Shop Polish, Fender's Pump Polish and Gibson's Pump Polish are all very good. For some time now, I have used Dunlop 65 cleaner, which is nice and light in its composition and therefore easy to use for cleaning and does not take ages to polish off with a cloth. There are so many brands and variants out there that each customer and owner is bound to have their favourites.

To clean up a guitar, take a non-abrasive polish and a cloth or towel, and spray the cleaner either directly on to the guitar or on to the cloth. It is more efficient to clean

OPPOSITE: A Gibson Les Paul Custom in for electric work.

Cleaning poly
or nitro with
Dunlop 65.

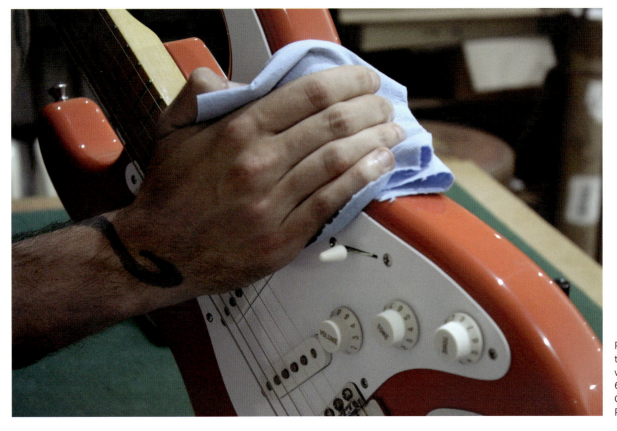

Polishing all
types of finish
with Dunlop
65 or a similar
Guitar Pump
Polish is safe.

A great look and feel once cleaned and polished.

Dunlop 65 is super easy to use and produces a great finish.

Virtuoso Polish & Cleaner gives superb results for nitro finishes.

up a whole guitar while the strings are off, either during the setup procedure or just during a string change. If you clean the string areas first – headstock and between the pickups, underneath the bridge, and so on – you will be able to get the new strings back on fairly swiftly, to allow the strings to settle in as well as the neck. You can then clean the rest of the guitar.

If a guitar has built up a significant amount of dirt and grime from years of gigging, with smoke, blood, sweat and tears, it may need something more than a standard pump polish. One product worth considering is Virtuoso Polish & Cleaner, which comes as a set of two bottles. The product in the first looks like an abrasive cleaner, although it does not have any cutting agent in it. It sorts out issues with a hazy or dull finish extremely well, but it can take some time to work. Once you have started the cleaning it is important to persist until the entire body or neck is done, as the area that has been worked can look quite different from untreated areas. When the cleaning has been done, it is time to apply the polish from the second bottle, which is more like a cream. This can be used quite sparingly as it travels around the surface of the guitar very well. After buffing with a good cloth, the finish will be brought back to a lovely shine.

The end result of all this cleaning and polishing is well worth the elbow grease. The two-part Virtuoso process can return a dull nitro finish to original showroom condition and make quite an impact on a guitar. The polished look is not for every-body, though. Some players definitely prefer the natural aged look, so, before committing fully to a Virtuoso treat-ment on a customer's guitar, it is worth double-checking that they really do want a high shine!

CHAPTER 11

Re-Stringing

String gauges and changes

The gauge of the strings on a guitar matters in many ways. Any difference in tension can have a significant effect on play and feel, neck relief, action height and intonation. Changing the strings regularly helps with all of the above and is crucial to getting the best setup out of the instrument. Spending time on getting all the setup points as right as they can be and then re-stringing well really adds to the overall feel and outcome of a good setup. Old strings can show a different tension in the neck, which in turn could throw the action height out a little. Really dirty strings will not intonate very well, if at all.

Many years ago, I was given an Epiphone ES335 to service and set up. Once the relief and action heights had been set, I checked the intonation. With the old strings on, the intonation of the High E was very flat at the 12th fret. Moving straight on and adjusting this, by sending the saddle forward to its max reach, I

found that it was still flat, with no more space for the saddle to go forward. After muttering to myself that the bridge must have been incorrectly placed, I decided to go ahead and change the strings and perhaps discuss tuning options with the owner later. After re-stringing, stretching the strings in and double-checking all the setup numbers, it was time to see just how much the intonation was out. There was nothing wrong with it! In fact, the saddle on the High E had to be screwed back to past its starting point. The problem was that the original string had been too old and was not resonating as it should, which was putting the intonation way out. It was another reminder always to change the strings for that final accurate check as well as for the overall feel of the instrument. This is why I do not check the intonation of a guitar when it first comes in for a setup. If the strings are old, it will probably be out; if any change to the setup points is needed, it will be out too. Changing the strings regularly not only helps with

getting the best setup and having the guitar feeling really good the majority of the time, but also allows you to maintain the guitar well.

There are many ways to re-string a guitar and all are effective, as long as there is a good amount of wrap around the tuning post, the string is wrapped tightly, making it look purposeful and deliberate, and there is a good break angle behind the nut that allows the strings to have a great lead out of the nut. This is the most important part.

There are good reasons for the first two elements. If the string is tight around the tuning post there is less chance of it slipping through play, which means better tuning stability. With a uniform amount of wrap around the tuning post, not only is the angle consistent but it also looks purposeful – a sleight of hand trick that reinforces the fact that the person who re-strung the guitar knows what they are doing! If there are variations in the amounts of wrap around the tuning posts, with some strings going the wrong way, it does not

OPPOSITE: Gibson ES390: a great smaller-sized semi-hollow.

instil confidence when the player looks down the neck at the headstock. When I returned from my studies in the USA, and set about sorting out many friends' guitars, they often remarked on the fact that the strings were all uniform, with the same amount of wrap around each tuning post. People are less likely to notice any alterations to the neck relief, action height, saddles or radius, or the cleaning out of all that gunk from the pots – all of which are so important. No, they always comment on how the strings are so nicely wrapped! Clearly, it matters to them aesthetically, but that is not the only reason why a good tech will always do it in the same way. Some touring techs may do it the same every time because of superstition, or because it is the way someone showed them many years ago, or perhaps because of time constraints. They understand the *how* of re-stringing, but not necessarily the *why*.

Re-stringing techniques and tips

There are typically two types of head-stock and machine head arrangement for both electric and acoustic guitars: 3 x 3, meaning three machine heads on either side of the headstock, or six-inline (where all the machine heads are in line). The aim should be to have the same amounts of wrap around the tuning post, as well as a good break angle with both, but there are different ways to measure to ensure you get the right amount of wrap around the post.

Nearly all Gibson electric and acoustic guitars (apart from Trini Lopez/Dave Grohls 335s and Firebirds, which are six-inline) have 3 x 3 headstocks. Most examples of this type of guitar also have a break angle in the neck and headstock.

Tales from the tours

Speed and efficiency can be very important on tour. A few years ago, two great touring guitar techs came to do a three-day build course, to brush up on some skills. Matt and Hoppy worked with the band Coldplay. (Matt's book *Roadie: My Life on the Road with Coldplay* is a great read for any aspiring touring guitar tech.) Towards the end of Day 2, the guitars were all at the point of being ready for the final assembly on Day 3. All that was left was to string up, and allow the strings, springs and neck relief to settle in overnight. I remember dis-cussing the amount of wrap, the string being tight around the tuning post and the angle behind the nut being very important, as well as the aesthetics, and then I went to put the kettle on. When I returned after no more than three minutes, both techs had finished stringing up their guitars! I am not sure the kettle had even boiled. The strings were strung up very well, with great wraps and angle. Their explanation for being so quick was that on the road

they needed to get the job done so that they could get their dinner! It does not take long to do a good re-stringing job; with regular practice, it can be very speedy.

Superstition often also comes up in conversation with touring techs. If they have re-strung a guitar in a certain way, including stretching in the strings, and the artist did not break a string, then that would usually be the way they would do it again and again and again – sometimes for years!

A very influential lecture in the USA in 2006 at the Gibson Custom Shop Summer Jam, given by a touring tech of 20 years, taught me a lot about superstition in re-stringing, about con-sistency, and about working for profes-sional guitarists. Being responsible for a guitarist breaking a string could be a sackable offence. Not only are the break angle, the tightness of the wrap-ping around the tuning post and the aesthetics important, it is also important not to get fired! Not all professionals on tour would dismiss their tech if a string broke in front of 80,000 people on the first chord, but some certainly did.

The 3 x 3 machine-head arrangement found on nearly all Gibsons and derivatives.

Six inline vintage-style machine heads.

Six inline modern-style machine heads.

PRS locking-style machine heads.

This is usually 14 or 17 degrees, meaning that the strings will naturally have a good angle down behind the nut and therefore have a good lead out of the nut. This does not mean that the strings do not need to be wrapped well around the tuning post, but it is not as imperative as with a six-inline. All the reasons for a good amount of wrap – a purposeful look, tight wrapping around the post for better tuning stability, and a good break angle – are still valid, even with the angled headstock.

With an electric guitar that has three machine heads per side and a bridge/tail-piece arrangement, such as the Gibson Les Paul, it is a good idea to put the strings through the tailpiece away from the body to reduce the risk of scratching the guitar's top. When strings have been put through with the tailpiece in place, it is not uncommon to see minor scratches on the Les Paul styles, where the strings have touched the top. Care should also be taken not to scratch the headstock. With all the strings in the tailpiece, bring the tailpiece to the studs on the body and place the strings over to the treble side.

Another good tip is to line up all the eyelet holes in the machine-head posts so that the strings all pass through very easily and not at differing angles, which can add to the confusion as to which way round the strings should go. Generally, this will make it quicker to get the string through and correctly measured.

The strings are put through the tailpiece and laid to one side.

Eyelet holes all lined up.

Bass E string

Starting with the Bass E string, thread the string through the hole and pull tightly with your thumb and forefinger behind the tuning post. Slide your thumb and forefinger the length of one and a half tuning posts down the string, and put a kink in the string. This measurement, once wrapped around the tuning post, should give you approximately three wraps around the tuning post.

Pull a very small amount of the string out of the tuning post so that, once the

Measuring the Bass E string one and a half tuning posts.

Putting a kink in the Bass E string.

Leaving a little bit of the Bass E string out, ready to cut off.

string is nicely wrapped around the tuning post and close to pitch, you will be able to cut it off at a nice 90-degree angle. This also reduces the risk of you damaging the headstock face with the string cutters. All you will touch is the washer and/or bushing rather than some lovely lacquer.

With the string now measured, try and hold it with the excess past the kink you have made upright, and then, with a string winder and your right hand gently holding the string, start to turn the machine head in an anti-clockwise direction. Once the string starts to bend around the tuning

post, gently increase the pressure, pulling the string back with your right hand.

Once the string has turned the corner you can pull right back with the right hand and the string will stay there. This will ensure that the string is constantly tight around the tuning post; keeping the

Winding the Bass E string.

The Bass E string going over the top.

Using a string winder.

pressure on by pulling back with your right hand really helps. A good tip here is to point your right-hand index finger down behind the nut at the same time as pulling back on the string.

The string and the kink that you have put in will go over the top of the string as you continue to turn the machine head, ideally with a string winder and in an anti-clockwise direction. Once the kink has gone over and with continued pressure with the right hand pulling back, you can continue to wind. The string will wrap around the tuning post and go down the post, creating that break angle. It is good practice not to allow the string to glide all the way through the nut while it is being strung up; heavier-wound strings will score the nut slot a little and over time could cause the nut to 1st fret height to lower, possibly creating some overtones or fret buzz off the 1st fret.

With the string nicely and tightly wrapped around the post and almost at pitch (usually done by ear), you can relax the pressure with the right hand and the wrap should remain tight. Be careful not to relieve the pressure too soon, otherwise the coil you have made might unravel itself and cause a gap around the post.

A string

Moving on to the A string, place the string through the post hole, pulling it tight, and again measure one and a half tuner posts with your thumb and forefinger. This requires an element of guess work as you can only measure past the D machine head, but it is quite easy to see one and a half lengths and, with the strings now getting thinner than the heavy Bass E string, there is a touch more tolerance to the measurement. Once you

Pressure is applied to ensure the string is tight around the tuning post.

Bass E string with three nice wraps around the tuning post.

Bass E string cut with the string cutters.

A string winder can be used with a hand drill for swift changes, but there is a risk of breaking the string.

D string with uniform wraps.

are happy with the distance, bring the string back to the tuning post and put a kink in it. Place a little of the string back through the post so that you can cut it off cleanly once it is close to pitch, and then start to wind slowly with the string winder. Once the kink goes over the string, you are free to start winding. Take up the pressure with your right hand too.

Once the string is getting close to pitch and is nicely wrapped down around the tuning post, you can take the pressure off and let it pull up close to pitch in the nut slot without holding it.

D string

Measuring the D string is slightly different as you cannot measure one and a half tuner posts past the D machine head. However, you can pull the string back one and a half tuning posts. So, with the string through the hole in the tuning post use your right hand to pull the D string back to half-way between the A and E post, the same one and a half posts distance, and then put a kink in it. Now push the string back through the hole and leave a little exposed so that you can cut it off once it is fully wrapped. Continue winding as you did with the E and A strings.

G, B and treble E string

The G string is usually the first unwound string, so it can be slightly trickier to sort out as the unwound strings can easily slip out of the tuner post hole, up to the point at which they have fully turned the corner. Because of this, it is necessary to apply a slightly more gentle pressure when pulling back, this time with the left hand.

G string measuring nearly two tuning posts.

A little string is left out so that it can be cut off squarely.

The hands are swapped around for the treble side.

The thumb can be used to apply and retain pressure on the string.

Swapping hands at this point really helps. Once you have measured it, as with the D string, you will find it much easier if you change hands and pull the string back through with your left and use the right to wind the string. Use your index finger to force the string down just behind the nut, encouraging the break angle. With the unwound strings you can be a little more liberal with the measurements. You should still aim for one and a half tuning posts, but you can add a little more due to the lack of thickness and wind on the unwound strings.

Continue with the B and E strings in the same way, swapping hands and measuring the same, continuing to get a good amount of wrap around and tightly down the tuning posts.

Alternative machine heads and methods

Locking machine heads became quite popular in the mid- to late 1980s, as use of the tremolo arm became more extreme. The aim of a locking machine head is to hold the string against the tuning post, usually with a pin that presses up against the string through the eyelet hole. Sending the string through the hole and then pulling tight while winding up the tuner sends the pin up and against the string, locking it in place. With less than a whole turn of the tuner, the string will be at pitch.

The locking machine head can allow a swift individual string change if at a gig, but there is downside to this type in the lack of a break angle, with the string not going down the tuner post. Sometimes, six-inline headstocks with locking machine heads can have some open-string buzzing where the string angle out of the nut is not acute enough, as there is no wrap around the post. Measuring the string in a similar way as for a standard machine head (for six-inline measuring three machine heads) can achieve a few wraps and a better angle. The string is still locked in and wrapping will help the angle. Sometimes, however, this is not possible. With a staggered machine-head post – essentially where the amount of wrap around the tuning post is reduced as the strings progressively get smaller – it is only possible to get a couple of wraps around the tuning post.

B string with nice wraps.

Drill and winder on the High E string.

All six strings wrapped nicely, ready for stretching in.

Pitching

Once all the strings are on, it is time to get them to pitch, starting with the bass strings and working from Bass E to Treble E. By the time you get to the High E and then come back to the Bass E you can expect it to have gone flat as the neck relief pulls and the strings are stretching in. Continue to bring the strings up to pitch until you get back to the Bass E and it is pretty much stable. That is good enough for now!

Stringing an acoustic guitar

Most electric owners will also have an acoustic guitar, so it is worth adding a note about stringing this type. The process is very similar to stringing an electric 3 × 3, although it does require a slightly different technique to get the strings well placed within the bridge slots and between the bridge pins. There are a few tools that can help with re-sizing the bridge pin posts but essentially it is about getting the ball end of the strings to sit well, up against the bridge plate inside the box. The bridge plate usually touches the 'X' brace on the underside of the top of an acoustic guitar and therefore transfers the tone, so it is very important to get the strings sitting well.

Starting with the Bass E, place the string down the string hole in the bridge and place the bridge pin over it and down into the string hole. Pull up on the string and gently push down with the bridge pin until you feel the ball end of the string and the bridge pin meet. This will seat the ball

end correctly on the bridge plate. Once the strings are all in place, the stringing-up method is more or less the same as for an electric guitar. However, it is worth considering that the more standard string gauge on an acoustic guitar would be a set of 12s, as opposed to, say, 10s on the electric, so when winding the Bass E up you might want to measure slightly less than one and a half tuner posts. Ending up with two to three wraps around the post is perfectly sufficient for a good break angle.

Case study: stringing a six-inline with vintage-style machine heads on a Stratocaster

Fenders and all their derivatives typically have six-inline machine heads, but there are a few different types of machine head in this configuration. This Stratocaster has the vintage-style tuners that are to be found on many Fenders. The machine heads usually have a split post and the

Vintage-style tuners in a Fender custom shop.

string drops into the hole in the post and is then wound up to pitch.

On modern Fenders, the string is sent through the eyelet hole of the machine head and measured in the same way, to achieve a uniform amount of wrap around the tuning post. It is more crucial on this style of guitar that you get a good break angle off the back of the nut. The strings going down the tuning post will mean they lead better out of the nut, preventing any open-string overtones or buzzing. If you can hear some of this on the open string, there is not enough of a break angle behind the nut. In my experience, this can occur especially on a G string, where the headstock does not have a string tree (retainer) on the G and D strings, or where the string has not been wrapped around the tuning post very well. If there is not enough wrap, the open string may buzz a little – this can be easily fixed with a few more wraps around the post, or sometimes with a little cleaning of the nut with some 320-grit sandpaper folded in half. In most cases, simply swapping out the string that is buzzing and making sure it is correctly strung will help a great deal.

To re-string a guitar with the vintage-style machine heads, start by threading all the strings through the bridge. Some strings will get stuck or hit the underside of the bridge plate, so it is usually easier to have the guitar on the bench and resting on your shoulder, then move it away from you so you can see the hole in the bridge for each string. Carefully push the first string through and then repeat for all six strings in that position. Once they are all through, pull them up, ensuring that the ball end of the string is fully inside the bridge block and not just hanging. If this happens, when you are getting the string closer to pitch, it will fall off the bridge block edge and you will have to make more

All the strings threaded through the bridge.

wraps than you have measured for. Always remember to double-check that the ball ends are within the bridge.

With the guitar now on its back on the bench and neck support, start with the Bass E string. Pull the string up and, with your left-hand thumb and forefinger holding the string, pinch it just at the tuning post and slide along the string the length of three machine heads. Rather than put a kink in it, as you would with a 3 × 3 or the modern six-inline configuration,

cut the string here with the string cutters, then place it inside the post and send it to the bottom of it. There are openings on either side of the post and the string can be bent over these and pulled back gently with the right hand, enabling you to get a good tight wrap around the pot. Using your right hand, point the string down behind the nut, pulling back a little at the same time. Using a string winder, start to wind the string on to and around the tuning post, sending the string lower down the more you wind and keeping the string taut with the right hand. A minimum of three wraps around the post will create a good break angle behind the nut, giving a better and cleaner open note. This will not only prevent buzzing or overtones but may also aid the open-chord intonation. If the string is buzzing in the nut, it is not leading out of the leading edge properly and therefore the distance between the nut and first fret will be longer, causing it to lead off sharp.

Measuring the Bass E string three tuning posts.

Cutting the string.

Placing the string directly in the tuning-post hole.

Bending the string over.

Bass E string fully wrapped.

Continuing with the A and D strings, measure three tuner posts and cut the strings at that distance. When you get to the first of the unwound strings, the G string, you will have to guesstimate a minimum of three tuner post lengths by sliding your thumb and forefinger down the string, past the B and E tuners, plus an imaginary post. Alternatively, you could use your right hand and pull the string back three tuner posts. A good point to remember here is that the G string is not only the first of the unwound strings but also the string with the least amount of break angle behind the nut, the next two being the High B and E, which tend to have a string tree (usually a small T-shaped retainer that holds both strings closer to the headstock, creating a better angle behind the nut). This is the reason why the amount of wrap around the tuning post, particularly with the G string, is so important to gain a good angle and improve the open-note articulation. A little bit of back filing of the nut can help (*see* Chapter 14), but it is ensuring that there is a good amount of wrap and wrapping the string down the tuning post that are vital.

Using a drill with the string winder makes for swift changes.

D string with uniform wraps.

B string: it is important to have a good amount of wrap.

E string.

For the B and E strings, pull the string back with the right hand and measure at least three tuning post lengths, or maybe even four. As with the G string and the unwound strings on a 3 × 3 style head-stock, these require a little less pressure when winding as they will easily slip out or just pull out of the tuner post. The High B and E break angle is improved by the string tree. If you want to hear what the strings sound like without this retainer, just lift them out from under it. In most cases, they will have a slight overtone or, worse, they will be buzzing off the nut. Some guitars with a similar headstock design may have a string tree on the D and G strings, due to the break angle being even more shallow behind the nut.

String trees

A string tree is a very inexpensive way of getting a break angle and will be found more commonly at the lower end of the market. This is because the necks on less expensive guitars are made from thinner wood, which allows the manufacturer to cut more from one piece of material. No doubt this is how Leo Fender designed it, to get a few necks out of one billet of wood. The alternative is something like the much more costly one-piece mahogany neck that was a feature of Gibson guitars at the time.

There is some debate about the friction caused by a string tree and one example of a Fender that does not have string trees is the Eric Johnson signature Strat. Eric Johnson did not want anything touching the strings that could cause friction, so this guitar started with a thicker piece of wood to create the better, deeper break angle behind the nut. Fender came up with a roller string tree to help aid any movement underneath.

Eric Johnson's approach to his signature Strat may have been because the majority of the six-inline headstock types usually come with a tremolo and floating bridge. When used, this essentially moves the strings forwards and backwards over the nut as well as anything in their way. A string tree can hinder the freedom of that movement and could end up being a small factor in a lack of tuning stability.

Nice uniform string wraps.

Strings ready for some stretching.

Stretching the strings in

Once all the strings are nicely strung and at the pitch of the player, it is very useful to get them stretched in. The aim of stretching the strings in is so that they reach an optimum tuning stability. The extent of stretching that needs to be done will come down to how quickly you need the strings settled. If the guitar is to be gigged or used in a recording studio, ideally it should be re-strung the night before at least. If time does not allow for this, stretching the strings in will achieve better stability more quickly.

More often than not, with the turn-around of most setup and repairs in the workshop being about seven to fourteen days, the strings can be allowed to settle in over a reasonable period of time. Just before it is collected, the guitar's tuning is double-checked and it is re-tuned as necessary; usually, the strings are a little flat a few days after a re-string. Playing the guitar to check its playability, and bending the strings will stretch them and stabilise the tuning before its owner comes to collect it.

One way of stretching the strings is to pull each string up individually about three-quarters of an inch around the pickup area and then try and fret each note by sliding your fretting finger up the fretboard from 1st fret to last. Do this for every string of the fresh set and then double-check the tuning. This usually shows that they have flattened by at least a semi-tone. As you repeat the process, you should see a gradual tendency for the strings to be less flat, which indicates that they are stretching and settling. This can be done until the strings are only a little flat. The other part to this process is to gently bend the strings over any break angle – at the nut to 1st fret as well as behind the nut and also over the bridge saddles. If there are any issues with one of these break angles or any issue with a string, then the string would break at that point and could be replaced straight away, rather than waiting until after the artist has played their first chord on stage.

If you are setting up the guitar for someone who will be on stage that night, or maybe the next night, getting the strings stretched and well settled in will be of great benefit and should reduce the possibility of any tuning when they come to perform. Most players who are having their guitars re-strung the night before or on the day of a performance will be going through a number of guitars and, in this case, the string stretching is done to last a few songs. However, most customers who bring their guitar to a workshop to be set up or re-strung will probably have that set of strings on for much longer. In this case, stretching the strings in so much that they are great for one or

Stretching the strings in: the right hand pulling the string up

...and the left hand fretting up the neck.

Stretching the strings can help settle them in more quickly.

two performances is not appropriate. It makes sense for a touring tech to know how to get strings nicely settled in when a gigging guitarist is going to attack them for a few hours straight, but if this was done for every guitar setup, the average customer would not be very happy. It can affect the elasticity and limit the life of the strings and players who enjoy their guitars fairly regularly could find the strings falling off from their prime a touch too quickly.

Getting the setup correct and the strings settled in over a few days, and double-checking the guitar before it leaves the workshop has always worked very well, and I have never had a customer complain that the strings were not settled in enough. This may not be the case with a performing artist, though, so it is important for a tech to have an understanding at least of how to get strings stretched in.

Getting the strings nicely wrapped has many positive effects and should be an essential skill for any guitar tech. The method of stringing is not really important, as long as the key points are covered: break angle, a good amount of wrap, and that all-important aesthetic.

CHAPTER 12

Pickup Heights

Understanding pickup heights, volume and tone

There are many different opinions about how to get the best volume and tone out of pickups, and it is always going to be a subjective topic of discussion. However, there are a few constant factors that need to be considered.

Some manufacturers give specifications on heights, and these are always a good place to start. Specs provided by reputable pickup makers are also invaluable.

Pickup heights (with the string fretted at the 21st fret)

Fender $4/32$in bass side, $3/32$in treble side

Gibson   Neck pup bass and treble side $3/32$in

Bridge pup bass and treble side $1/16$in
With the pickups closer to the strings, there will be more volume and power, but possibly less clarity. With the pickups lower, there will less volume, but the tones will be cleaner.

Always fret the last fret when checking and adjusting the pickup heights.

OPPOSITE: Setup work on a Gibson Les Paul Standard '56 reissue.

Manufacturers' specs are absolutely fine for nearly all customers, although checking the balance between bridge and neck pickup on a guitar with two humbuckers is essential. Having a nice balance of the bridge pickup and neck when together will give that sweet humbucker sound.

For single-coil pickups it is also necessary to get the in-between positions, either the middle selection on a Telecaster-style guitar or positions 2 and 4 on a Strat-style, sounding nicely balanced. The aim is a pleasing tonal range rather than a volume range. Typically, with Strats, with the setup points complete, playing a few bar chords and going from the neck position on the 5-way switch through to the bridge, the tone should change uniformly between each pickup. There should also be a nice balance between the bass and treble range of the pickup.

Adjusting the pickups

To adjust the pickups either up or down to meet the manufacturer's or maker's heights, first make sure that all the setup points are complete. Fret the string at the last fret (21st or 22nd, or maybe even the 24th) and place the 6in ruler on either the pole piece or the pickup cover. Measuring from the top of the pickup to the underside of the string, adjust the pickup height screw, tightening it to raise the pickup height or loosening it to lower. Note that the bass and treble heights are different from one another on most single coils, while on humbuckers they are usually the same. Most pickup height screws require a Phillips screwdriver, while some vintage pickups or re-issue pickups will use flat-head screws. Always

Stratocaster pickup heights: fretting the 21st fret.

...the pickup height is ⁴/₃₂in.

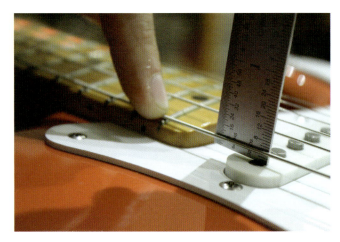

Measuring from the pole piece bass side...

Measuring from the pole piece treble side...

...the pickup height is ³/₃₂in.

Pickup height adjustment screws.

check the output and tonal range through an amp.

Sometimes, the pickup heights can be dialled in to suit the player's style, their amp and/or their pedals. As an example, if they have a particularly bright rig then the pickups slightly lower on the treble side could help; however, this is only with a clear understanding of the player's rig, which is not always possible. If you are adjusting pickup heights for yourself and know how you like to dial in a specific pickup to a tone, this is a very fulfilling activity, and will ideally result in a great balance. If you are working on a guitar that belongs to someone else, in most cases the best you can do is refer to the specs. In almost all setups, meeting the manufacturer's specifications will work well, but very occasionally – perhaps for a touring musician – the heights might need triple-checking.

Full Setup, Start to Finish: Gibson Les Paul Standard

Following a complete setup, from initial assessment to handing back to the customer, of a modern Gibson Les Paul – a guitar of the fixed-bridge style with 3 × 3 machine heads. It was a player's guitar that had not been set up or serviced for a while and was due a good pro setting up, and a full treatment following all the maintenance points.

The first action is to tune up to the pitch of the player. The Gibson Les Paul is to be set at standard pitch and it is worth noting that the string gauge is going to be 0.010in–0.046in, which is the gauge of the strings that are currently on the guitar. The condition of the strings on the guitar is good enough to be able to assess its setup points as well as to make any adjustments. The player's style is rock and blues, so they need a good playable guitar, with nice clean notes for open-chord playing, an ease of play up the neck, and strings that can be bent, for some blues lead playing.

Playing and assessing the guitar

With the guitar tuned up well, it is always worth taking the time to play it prior to assessing the setup points. When a customer brings a guitar in for a service, they will often tell you what is wrong with it, but it always helps to play it yourself, to see whether you come to the same conclusion or at least to understand where they might be coming from. It can be a mistake

Gibson Les Paul Standard '58 reissue.

to go straight to the issue they are having and try to fix that, without going back to square one and following the assessment and setup procedure methodically. An issue with intonation is a good example of this, as so many factors can affect this.

Playing some open chords will potentially highlight any nut to 1st fret issues, open-chord intonation issues (often related to incorrect neck relief), general string height and playability. Playing some bar chords up the neck around the 5th to 7th fret will feed back how comfortable the guitar is to play. If the chording is difficult, it could be an issue with the neck relief or the bridge height (which might be too high). If the strings are buzzing around the middle area of the neck, this could be related to a combination of too little relief and the bridge height being too low.

The Gibson Les Paul feels and sounds fine when playing open chords and bar chords up the neck, although they do become a little trickier further up the neck. There is a sense that the string height is a touch too high for real ease of play. There are some very slight tuning issues between certain open chords: the G chord sounds good as do the C and D, but the A chord sounds slightly out. This is fairly common and could be related to the neck causing a higher nut to 1st fret.

Moving up the neck and into some lead playing, with some bending of the strings there is a sense that they will go over the fingers when the playing is aiming for large tone and half-step bends. Attacking the B string for one of these bends at the 15th fret does indeed make the G string slide over the top of the fingers, which is not very comfortable and would indicate either too much neck relief or bridge height. The notes do not choke out,

though. They resonate well and it is possible to get some vibrato on top of the bend, so it is probably not a fret issue. It is more likely to be related to something within the setup of the guitar. The intonation higher up the fretboard sounds a little out but, given that there is already a feeling that the guitar's neck relief is not quite right, this is probably nothing to worry about at this stage. There is a lot of setting up to do first. Quite often, once the various setup adjustments have been made, the intonation will come good.

Playing the guitar and getting a feel for these setup points, as well as maybe making sense of the customer's perspective of how the guitar plays, is a great start. Playing the guitar through an amp can then highlight a few maintenance points – rolling down the volume and tone pots to listen for any crackling, and carrying out a little initial assessment of pickup heights by switching between the rhythm and treble positions on the 3-way.

After playing and assessing the guitar, the conclusion is that it is resonant and sustains well. There are some minor open-chord intonation issues, a lack of ease playing up the neck, and some string-height issues when bending notes, although they do sustain. There is also some crackling in the volume pots. A visual inspection determines that the fretboard is dirty but not too bad, the frets would definitely benefit from some fret polishing and there is the usual dulling of the lacquer where the right forearm rests. The back of the neck is also a little dull from playing, while the hardware looks OK but is a little dull too, as the nickel naturally ages and loses its brightness over time. Some general cleaning up will bring the guitar back to a nice condition.

Mapping out the setup points

After the initial assessment, the setup points need to be mapped out, starting with the neck relief.

The guitar is brought carefully off the neck support on the bench and the neck is held in the left hand. The notched straight edge is held gently between thumb and forefinger in position between the D and G strings, the straight edge resting on the 2nd fret. With the guitar closer to the eye, it is possible to view the gap between the straight edge and the fretboard. There is a little bit of light, so the neck is definitely in relief. With a 0.016in feeler gauge slid between the fretboard and the straight edge at the 7th fret, there is still some light and the feeler gauge is not touching the notched straight edge. A 0.020in feeler gauge does touch the notched straight edge and fretboard – clear from the sound of the metal feeler gauge against the metal edge – but there is still some space between the two. Using a 0.022in feeler gauge, the sound is much more consistent with the feeler gauge touching the fretboard and the notched straight edge. This 0.022in neck relief is recorded on the setup points sheet.

To look at the action height, the 6in steel rule with 32nds and 64ths is placed on the 12th fret. Measuring between the top of the fret and the underside of the string, the bass-side action height is at $\frac{4}{32}$in and the treble side $\frac{3}{32}$in.

The measurements recorded on these first two setup points reflect the outcome of the playing assessment: with too much relief in the neck, the string height is too high, affecting the playability and causing the strings to go over the bending fingers. It also highlights why the guitar is particularly resonant, as the strings have quite

Measuring the neck relief.

Gibsons have a $5/16$in nut; anyone who does not have a $5/16$in nut more than likely does not have a Gibson.) With the nut wrench placed on the brass nut of the truss rod at the 10 o'clock position, and with the guitar safely on the bench and in the neck support, the truss rod is tightened to the 2 o-clock position. With the guitar still on the bench and in the neck support, the tuning is checked. The majority of the strings will have gone slightly sharp, bass side more than treble. Each string is slackened off and then brought back up to pitch. Positioning the notched straight edge back on the fretboard and bringing the guitar up to the eye, it is slightly noticeable that the gap between the fretboard and the rule has reduced. A 0.016in feeler gauge at the 7th fret only just goes between the two – it is a tight fit, but the notched straight edge does not knock or fall on to the board, indicating that the neck relief has reduced by 0.006in. Removing the nut wrench and re-positioning back to the 10 o'clock position and supporting the guitar on the bench with the right hand on the neck, the truss rod is tightened again from 10 to 2. The adjustment is now getting very tight but there is no cause for alarm yet. Checking the tuning shows that the strings are now sharp, quite consistently across the board.

With the strings slackened, just down a semi-tone and then re-tuned, the relief is checked again. With the notched straight edge on the board, a visual check confirms that the gap between the rule and the fretboard is very slight. A 0.010in feeler gauge slides easily between the rule and the fretboard. There is the slightest bit of light visible but there is an audible sound of the metal gauge against the notched straight edge on the fretboard. The neck

a bit of height to move. It is something worth keeping in mind. If the overall playability improves, but the guitar still lacks resonance or sustain, it may be worth points trying to reach a middle ground, but that will be best determined once the setup and even all the maintenance points have been completed.

The nut to 1st fret height is checked with the feeler gauges carefully slid between the top of the fret and under the string, without moving the string. Approached from the bass side and then the treble, the measurement is at 0.022in bass side, going down to 0.020in treble side. Sliding a 0.020in feeler gauge under the strings, putting some radius on to it

and then pulling in both sides with thumb and forefinger and then over the fret, shows that the strings are slightly over the gauge. Some light shows underneath on the bass side but the gauge is touching the unwound treble strings. This nut to 1st fret height is consistent with having too much neck relief and should improve as the setup is adjusted.

Adjusting the neck relief and the action height

With these points mapped out, it is time to get the neck relief and the truss rod adjusted with a $5/16$in nut wrench. (All

Measuring the action heights.

relief target on this setup is 0.008in at the 7th fret. This will accommodate the player's style well, giving enough relief to play some open chords with a degree of attack. It will be comfortable up the neck for some pentatonic scales and the neck will also be straight enough for some lead playing, matched with a ⁵⁄₆₄in bass-side action height and ⁴⁄₆₄in on the treble side. Another small tightening of the truss rod should get the neck relief to the right place, at 0.008in. After tightening the truss rod and checking the tuning, some strings required a little attention: flattening and then bringing them back up to pitch should allow enough time for the neck to settle. Using the notched straight edge and the 0.008in feeler gauge at the 7th

fret between the rule and the fretboard, the gauge fits very well between the two, without any knocking or too much scraping. The first adjustment to the setup is now complete.

Before playing the guitar – and resisting this is sometimes hard to do – the action height at the 12th fret as well as the 1st fret needs to be considered and adjusted where necessary. With the straighter neck – the relief is now lower, at the desired point of 0.008in – the action height should also have improved. A check shows that it has reduced to ³⁄₃₂in bass side and ²⁄₃₂in treble, a reduction of ¹⁄₃₂in each side. Although this is an acceptable action height at the 12th fret, the aim here is to optimise playability for an owner

whose style is to be not too heavy on the open attack and who wants the playing to be relatively easy. Because of this, the action height for the bass side needs to be lowered slightly, by ¹⁄₆₄in, to ⁵⁄₆₄in. An ESP multi-spanner is used to lower the bass-side thumb wheel on the Tune O Matic bridge by a minor clockwise turn (a quarter of a turn on the wheel). Another check of the height at the 12th fret with the ruler gets the bass-side string to just the right place; on the rule, the line of ²⁄₃₂in and above will be seen, but not the line of ³⁄₃₂in. On the 64ths side, after some practice the bottom of the string lining up to the ⁵⁄₆₄th line on the rule is clear to see.

Following the slight lowering of the bridge, the strings have gone flat, so these need tuning up to pitch. This will re-establish the correct relief in the neck and is necessary to review the nut to 1st fret height. Using a 0.020in feeler gauge under the string and over the 1st fret, it is clear that the gauge is slightly too thick, but the 0.018in feeler gauge now fits snugly under the strings all across the fret. Because it has been measured beforehand, entering the feeler gauge from the bass-side E/A/D strings and then taking it out and around to the treble side is easier. It can also help with gaining an understanding of where the height is now. Placing the feeler gauge just behind the fret and putting a little radius into it by holding it with the thumb and forefinger indicates that 0.018in is the average across the nut to 1st fret height, on both bass and treble side.

The intonation of the guitar will be finalised once the new strings are on. It could be done before re-stringing, since all the setup points have been covered, but the guitar will need playing in a bit first to be sure that the setup is just right.

As it will be handed back to the customer with new strings on, intonating with those strings is best practice.

Checking playability

Once the key setup points have been covered and the tuning has been double-checked, it is time to assess the guitar's overall feel and playability. The condition of the existing strings is good enough to be able to get a feel for the setup points, and the tension in the neck and over the strings. With experience, even without the new strings you should be able to tell where the setup is. It should already feel much better.

It is quite noticeable that the strings feel much closer to the fretboard all the way up the neck, not just in any one area. The proportional string height feels so much better when playing open chords and bar chords up to the 12th fret. There is also still a good amount of sustain and resonance, positive attributes that the guitar had before, so it is good to hear that they have not gone away. The open chords sound better-tuned (just by ear) and the intonation sounds good over the 1st to 3rd fret as well as further up the neck. Notes that are bent up the neck, around the 7th to 9th fret, feel that they have a much nicer tension and the sense that the strings will go over the fingers has gone. Previously, this was subtle around this area but, as the strings did go over the fingers further up, there is always a possibility of them doing the same around the common pentatonic positions too. The tension in the string has definitely improved. When learning the theory of guitar setup, it can be difficult to grasp the fact that, with more tension in the truss rod and, therefore, a straighter neck, the overall tension in the string actually feels less. This is the case

even though every time it has gone sharp through the process, before being slackened off and re-tuned. There are a few reasons for this, and it is where the feel of the guitar comes back to its playability. With the neck being straighter, there is a better angle between the strings and the frets. An ever-increasing string height, once that is also set, allows the strings to vibrate freely and consistently over the entire fretboard.

Moving up the neck, the bends around the 12th and 15th positions do not choke any more. This aspect is always worth double-checking when straightening a neck and therefore essentially lowering the string heights. More importantly, the strings next to the note being bent no longer go over the fingers, which not only

feels uncomfortable but can also make a player lose confidence in the setup of the guitar. Once this issue has been sorted out, it inspires instant confidence in the guitar's playability, making aiming for some big tone-and-a-half step bends very easy, and ensuring that the guitar performs well. This is all a great improvement compared with how the guitar played and felt before – and there is still the re-stringing to come.

Cleaning

At this juncture it is time to carry out the maintenance steps of the setup.

Using a normal string winder, which will be perfectly adequate – or the

Playing the setup in and getting a feel for it.

StewMac string winder, adapted to make use of a hand drill for superior speed! – all the strings are slowly de-tuned and removed. With the strings slackened off on this style of bridge and tailpiece configuration, the tailpiece can slide off its studs and down the face of the guitar, so the tailpiece needs to be held with the right hand. Once the strings come cleanly out of the eyelet holes, the tailpiece and strings are removed, cut and then discarded in the bin.

With all the strings off, the fretboard can be cleaned using wire wool and oil soap, following the grain and moving up and down the neck as well as across. The dirt and grime will slowly lift off the board and the rosewood will start to look very good. The frets will also benefit from this, although going back over them with some 0000-grade wire wool and the fret guard will not only remove any residue of wood oil soap but also bring them to a nice shine. The frets higher up the fretboard and particularly on the bass side appear slightly more tarnished as they tend to have been played less, so polishing out all the frets all the way up the fretboard makes for an impressive-looking guitar. The feel of the nicely polished frets will make playing the guitar a much more pleasurable experience.

Before getting round the back and into the electrics to clean out those dirty pots, a fine brush is used to get rid of any dust around the hard-to-reach places whilst the strings are on the guitar. The area around the bridge and between the pickups, as well as the headstock, will all benefit from a dusting before cleaning. The bridge-height wheels will inevitably move but, as the neck relief is correct at pitch, restoring the bridge height to $\frac{5}{64}$in bass side and $\frac{4}{64}$in treble is relatively easy once the strings are all back on. If

moving the bridge wheels and having to re-establish the height causes any concern, the bridge can be held with one hand while carefully dusting with the other. This style of bridge will usually fall off when it is turned over to clean out the electrics, although the thumb wheels might not move. The best option is not to worry about them and trust the numbers.

The four screws securing the backplate are removed and Servisol switch cleaner is sprayed directly into each pot, to clean them out. The knobs can be turned while doing this, to get the cleaner working really well through the pot. To do this, the guitar will need to be on its side and resting in the neck support. After cleaning, the volume and tone pots are checked while the guitar is plugged into an amp, strumming all the strings at the same time as rolling down and turning both pots up and down. If the pots are nice and clean, there should not be any crackles.

The guitar can now be given a good clean using some Dunlop 65. The nitro-cellulose lacquer on the guitar is in pretty good shape, although it does have the usual marks and dullness around the playing positions. Spraying polish on to some blue workshop towel and gently rubbing on to the lacquer in circular motions will brighten these dull areas and easily remove marks from the top of the guitar. The sides, back and neck are cleaned in the same way. Some more effort may be required in the heel end of the neck, as it is quite common for this area to be very dull. Sometimes (although not on this setup), it can be a time saver to remove the machine heads to get to the back of the neck and the front headstock facing, to get that cleaned up well. This guitar did not require it, however.

Stringing up

The next jobs are to string up the guitar, stretch the strings in and check the intonation. Correct stringing up is another key factor in getting the best out of the setup of a guitar. With this 3×3 machine head configuration, the aim is to have three wraps around each tuning post, gaining a little more with the unwound strings, for tuning stability, the break angle behind the nut as well as for aesthetic reasons.

The strings are threaded through the tailpiece away from the guitar. Once they are all in, the tailpiece is placed on the studs, the bridge placed on the thumb wheels and the strings placed parallel to the neck on the treble side. Starting with the Bass E string, this is put through the eyelet hole and, measuring one and a half tuning posts, kinked, then pulled back and slowly wound up with the string winder. In this case, with each string on and slowly brought back up to pitch, the strings are stretched in a little and the intonation checked and adjusted. Usually, the guitar is placed in a rack and left to settle in overnight or for a few days. Pulling the string up around the pickups and then running the fretted string all the way up the neck stretches the strings in well; they will become at least a half-step flat. The string height or bridge height will need to be double-checked once the strings have settled at pitch; there is no need to double-check the neck relief, as it will have pulled back up to exactly where it was left with strings of the same gauge on. However, it is not a long job to triple-check that too!

Confirming that the setup points are again as desired, it is now time to intonate the guitar, back in the playing position. Playing the open Bass E string and then the fretted Bass E string at the 12th fret, the notes are the same, which means that they are intonated. This is performed on all the strings. As is quite common with intonation, some of the strings are out just a little, while some are perfectly fine.

Completing the setup

Now for the serious, but fun, bit: properly checking how the guitar plays out. The more you play the guitar, the more new things might jump out at you, but it is worth being slightly disciplined: play those open-chord positions, check the intervals and the open-chord intonation by ear, go further up the neck with some bar chords, feel how easy it is to play the guitar, again checking the intervals, and then move on to bending notes higher up the fretboard, always checking that there is no choking of the notes, and that the notes are clear and sustaining. With the fretboard nice and clean and the frets polished up well, the feel under the fingers is inspiring, the guitar plays superbly and makes the owner want to play the guitar for some time. Playing through an amp will help with checking that the pots have been cleaned out well, so that they are free from crackles. The pickups should sound good, with a nice balance between the bridge and neck pickup, and the middle position should sound terrific too.

The whole setup is completed by cleaning any fingerprints off the machine heads, bridge and tailpiece, as well as running dry blue workshop towel back around the guitar, so that it is completely free of any sign that it has been worked on. The philosophy of the Galloup school was to get the work done and get out like you had never been there. Achieving this certainly generates the wow factor. As the guitar is taken back by its owner, not only does it look a million bucks, but it also plays that way, and without any sign that any tech has even touched it. It is a great setup and hopefully the owner will be a loyal customer for a long time off the back of it.

Full Setup, Start to Finish: Fender Stratocaster

Following the complete setup of a modern Fender Stratocaster, an example of a floating-bridge guitar, with six individual saddles and six-inline machine heads. It was another player's guitar that had not been serviced for a while – time for a good pro setup and for covering all those maintenance points.

This is a nice modern Stratocaster tuned up to standard pitch and currently strung up with a set of 10-gauge strings, which, determined by eye and feel, are in reasonable condition. A brief conversation with the owner indicates that their style is mainly blues and hard rock. The guitar is not playing that well and there seem to be quite a few potential problems that will need to be mapped out. Some of these have been highlighted by the customer, and of course there is a temptation to go straight to those issues and try to sort them out before taking all the necessary measurements. Being told where the problem lies can make it easy to ignore the proper order of assessment and adjustment. Students on the setup course who are very familiar with their guitars sometimes declare that they know 'exactly' where the problem is and go ahead and try to correct that issue without following the right procedure. They then find that something else is out and they have to try to re-trace their steps, until they are really unsure of where the setup is. It is due to a forgivable lack of understanding about the knock-on effects of each adjustment. With this Strat (as will all the others), it is

An older Stratocaster (1963) in for setup.

important to go over all the setup points in order, mapping out the numbers and then making the adjustments one after the other.

The first thing to do, with the strings tuned to pitch, is to have a little play around the open-chord area, some bar chords up the neck and some lead around these areas, before heading up the fretboard with some bends, a tone bend and tone-and-a-half bends mainly on the G, B and E strings. In the open-chord position, the strings feel quite low. They are resonant, but not quite as loud as some recent Strats that have been set up. Assessed by ear, the intonation sounds OK; it is certainly not overly sharp. Some lead playing around this area is quite easy. Some very minor overtones are heard when digging in a little, which is quite common with a lower string height (action). Bar chords are quite easy, but further up the neck there is a sense of some intervals between strings being out of tune to each other, more than likely from fretting of some of the notes being a little easier in the centre of the board than on the outer strings. Again, this is probably due to a lower string height.

The radius of the fretboard is the next concern and, as this guitar has six individual saddles on the bridge, it is going to be imperative to check the saddle radius. Heading further up the neck and playing some bends on the unwound strings there is definitely some choking. The top of the bend is just not ringing out and in more

Checking the neck relief on the older Stratocaster.

than a few areas the notes are choking out completely. This could be due to a low string height or a few under-radiused saddles and it is possibly also worth looking at the frets for low spots, where some of the tops of the frets are flattened out.

Some of these issues have already been highlighted by the customer but there are a few other areas that need attention: the float of the bridge is very low, there is hardly any vibrato movement at all, and the customer would also like a little more lift, just for some palm vibrato. Overall, the playability of the guitar is just not right. It feels tight, even though the string height is low, and the owner's complaint that they just cannot quite get behind the string and play easily is certainly justified.

After double-checking the tuning again, it is time to measure the neck relief, with the notched straight edge carefully placed on the fretboard between the D and G strings, long (25.5in) scale facing towards you. With it placed at the 2nd fret there is hardly any light between the fretboard and the straight edge at the 7th fret; by eye, it would appear to be less than 0.008in, which is the standard for this type of player and guitar. A 0.004in gauge just goes through between the fretboard and edge. This amount of relief would be fine if the guitar was playing great but it could account for some of the issues that have been identified over the open-chord positions and up the neck. Measuring the action height at the 12th fret, on top of the fret and to the underside of the string, the bass-side measures ⁵⁄₆₄in and the treble side ³⁄₆₄in. Having the bass-side action at that height is a little too low for most players, especially if they want to attack the open E string and avoid getting any overtones off the 1st fret or higher up the fretboard. This would certainly need to be addressed for a predominantly blues player, where playing the open E and A strings is common. The

nut to 1st fret height measured with a feeler gauge is 0.016in both bass side and treble. This measurement is at the lower end of the spectrum and is more than likely in direct relation to the slightly low amount of neck relief.

Checking the radius of the fretboard by placing the radius gauge over the strings and pushing down around the 12th fret – an easy check that can be confirmed once the strings are off – shows that it is 9.5in, which is standard for this age and model of guitar. Placing the gauge nearer the bridge and on the outer E strings, it is easy to see that the four strings in the middle are not meeting it, indicating that the saddles are slightly under-radiused. This is reflected in the lack of playability over the fretboard and the higher notes choking on some pretty standard and important bends.

The float of the bridge is not really measurable. With the ruler at the back of the bridge and carefully placed on the body, it is barely possible to read that it has a ¹⁄₆₄th. It is probably less, although the bridge does make the strings slightly sharp when pulled back with the tremolo arm, but it is really very minimal.

A brief assessment of the maintenance points, before going on to get the setup improved, shows that the maple fretboard looks good. It is a little dirty around the open-chord positions, but nothing too unsightly. The frets are a little dull and would certainly benefit from a polish. Cosmetically, the guitar is in a decent condition, but a general clean-up would make it look terrific. With the guitar plugged back in, the volume pot is crackling as are the tone pots.

Moving on to the adjustments, a little more neck relief should allow the bass-side open strings to resonate better, give the nut to 1st fret a little more room and increase the string height further up the neck. The truss rod is located at the headstock end,

so there is no need to be whipping off the neck. Using a 4mm Allen key placed at 2 o'clock (when looking down the neck from the machine heads), and just resting against the D string, the truss rod is loosened to just past 12 o'clock, and maybe a little further. The truss rod may feel tight, but once it starts to turn, it will go easily to where it needs to be. Checking the tuning afterwards shows that the strings have all fallen flat, an indicator that the neck has relaxed a little. With the strings re-tuned and with the notched straight edge back on the fretboard, the distance would appear to be a little more – there is certainly more light coming through. The 0.008in feeler gauge slides in between the straight edge and the fretboard, albeit quite snugly, so it seems that small backing off of the truss rod has increased the neck relief to the desired level, for now. There will have been a knock-on effect on the action heights, both at the 12th fret and at the nut to 1st fret. Both were on the low side, which was limiting the playability and the amount of attack that the player could use. At this point, with a tight 0.008in of relief, it is best to continue with the rest of the setup points. The neck relief may well change with other adjustments.

Measuring the 12th fret action height with the 6in steel rule on the fret and up to the underside of the string, it is now at ⁵⁄₆₄in on the bass side and just under ⁴⁄₆₄in on the treble. Both of these are good, but it would be worth getting the treble raised up just a small amount, so the string is exactly at ⁴⁄₆₄in. The bass-side height might be enough to allow the string to resonate well and play out, and it can always be adjusted and raised a little if it proves not to be. Using the appropriate small Allen key, both grub screws in the bridge saddles on the treble side are turned clockwise a very small amount, at the same time holding the steel rule on the 12th fret to see when the string meets the exact height of ⁵⁄₆₄in. This raising of the saddle will have made the string sharp, so the E string is tuned down and then back up to pitch.

Before moving on to the remaining four bridge saddles and checking and adjusting their radius, it is worth checking where the nut to 1st fret height has landed with the increase in neck relief caused by the adjustment. Using the feeler gauges and choosing 0.018in, the gauge is slid carefully under the string and over the fret bass side. It just fits under the E, A and D strings and then is taken out and slid under the E, B and G strings. Again, it is very tight but with a very steady hand it does not move the strings. To check the radius at the 1st fret, the gauge is slid under the strings between the 1st and 2nd fret and then, with the radius put into the gauge by holding it either side of the fretboard, it is placed over the fret and under the string at the 1st fret. This shows that the nut to 1st fret height is pretty even across the strings, with the slightest gap on the bass strings and the treble being a touch lower. This is a little improvement that will help a lot with the open string movement as well as improving the feel of the open-chord positions, and allowing the fretting hand to get under the string a touch more.

With the neck relief and the action heights improved, it is time to adjust the bridge saddles and match the radius of the fretboard. With the guitar on the bench and the neck resting on the shoulder, sighting down the strings with the radius gauge (9.5in) resting on the two outer E strings, it is possible to see some light under the gauge on the four middle strings. Each one of these strings must be just touching the radius gauge. Using the small Allen key and starting with the A string, both grub screws are tightened until the string just

Checking for any choking by bending the strings.

touches the gauge. This is done on each bridge saddle and all the grub screws. The four central strings are now very sharp, so all of the strings are slackened off a little and then tuned back up to pitch. Any change in the saddle radius will upset the balance of the float of the bridge, so flattening and then retuning all the strings to pitch helps to obtain a good balance of string and spring tension, and therefore a stable float. After double-checking that the radius gauge is sitting nicely on all the strings and that all the strings rattle off the gauge, the radiusing of the saddles is complete. A quick look at the float of the bridge indicates that has gained a little. Another double-check of the tuning shows that the outer Es have flattened a little due to the bridge having more lift from the previously under-radiused saddles being raised

to meet the radius. All the strings are slackened off again and then brought slowly back up to pitch, allowing the bridge to pull up and meet string and spring tension. Only now is it worth re-measuring the float of the bridge. From the body and up to the underside of the bridge plate, the lift now measures ⅔₂in, which is a good height, allowing for a nice amount of vibrato and flattening the strings as well as being able to sharpen them too. Aesthetically, the bridge lift looks good – not too high or too low. This is not vital to the functionality, but it is an area to which most customers and players are drawn by eye, and is sometimes judged in this way.

At this point in the setup, it is better to jump straight to the maintenance points, leaving the intonation until the clean-up has been completed and the new strings have

been put on. It would be possible to do the intonation now and it would not cause any issues, but intonating with the new strings is preferable. If they are of the same gauge, they should intonate exactly the same way.

Having de-tuned the guitar with the string winder, the slackened-off strings are cut and pulled out of the tuner holes as well as back through and out of the bridge block. On some Strats, the back plate needs to be removed, but on this one the strings came out easily. Now is the time to remove the scratch-plate screws carefully and get inside and clean out the electrics. On a modern guitar, it is not vital to keep the screws in the same position as they come out of the scratch plate, as they are usually evenly worn. However, with a vintage or older guitar it is worth laying the screws out on the bench in the order in which they came out, so that they can go back into the same holes. Most live and earth wires from the jack socket, as well as the earth from the bridge claw, allow for the scratch plate to be carefully lifted, turned through 90 degrees and then placed into the cavity. This one is nice and easy. The neck support now behind the scratch plate will stop it falling over too. This allows easy access to all the pots.

A couple of the pots were crackly, so the effect of cleaning these out should be noticed and appreciated by the player. Squirting the contact cleaner directly into the pot while simultaneously turning the knob on the outside of the scratch plate will ensure that the cleaner gets all the way through and around the contacts, to make the pots crackle-free. With the scratch plate off, there is a good opportunity to clean off any dust or dirt from around the edge of where it has been, as well as just inside the bridge area. Once the plate is back on and screwed up, a drop of Dunlop 65 cleaner on towel again can be used to

The pickup heights are the last items to check.

gently clean the top of the scratch plate. This is an area that is rarely cleaned unless all the strings are off.

The back of the neck is rubbed gently with blue towel, just to remove dust and dirt, then the fretboard is liberally sprayed with the cleaner and then cleaned with a fresh piece of blue towel. The dirt around the open-chord positions cleans up well and the blue towel very lightly cleans up the frets, but they still need a good polish. Using 0000-grade wire wool and the fret guard to protect the fretboard, they are polished from the 1st fret all the way to the 21st, giving them a shine that will make the strings feel great over them. Finally, a quick dust around the headstock area with a soft brush removes any dust, followed by a clean-up with the blue towel around the back of the headstock and tuners. Sometimes, it is worth removing the tuners in order to get the headstock, as well as the machine heads themselves, really clean. On this guitar it is not really necessary.

Time to string up. With the guitar stood up at 90 degrees to the bench, all the strings are threaded through the bridge block, pulled up and given a little tug, to make sure the ball ends are nicely through the block. They are then laid to the treble side and the neck is placed back in the neck support on the bench. Starting with the Bass E, the string is pulled up to and through the eyelet hole and then, with thumb and forefinger on the string behind the tuner post, slid back three tuners' lengths to measure. A kink is put in the string at that point and then it is pulled back with the right hand, until the kink is just past the tuner post. With the remaining string past the kink pointing up, winding begins, keeping the string taut with the right hand. Once the string has started to go around the tuner post, more pressure is applied and the string is wound more quickly, as it winds down the tuner post. Once all the string has been wound, it is released and left slightly under pitch (tuned by ear only). The remaining strings are all done in the same way, with the unwound strings measuring a little more so that there is slightly more wrap around the post, just to ensure the break angle behind the nut is sufficient.

Once all the strings are on and up to pitch, it is time for some stretching in, to get fully behind the setup now rather than leaving the guitar in the rack overnight or for a few days to settle. Raising the string with the right hand at the neck/middle pickup area and then running the left hand fretting all the way up the neck with every string will stretch them in well. They will lose about a semi-tone, or just over. Once it has been re-tuned to pitch, it is time to get playing the guitar, to check out the setup, the pots and the general feel and playability.

The guitar plays very well. The open chords feel and sound good, and the open intonation as well as the clarity of the strings and notes off the nut are also good. Playing up the neck, bar chords are comfortable. The proportional string height instantly and intuitively feels right, with each fretted area requiring the same amount of pressure, which makes for better-sounding chords and intervals. When bending the B and G strings around the 7th to 9th fret, the tension feels nicely balanced – they are easy to bend but with some resistance. Going further up and doing some tone-and-a-half step bends, the notes are clear and ringing out, with no choking – always a joy to hear when there was some choking beforehand. The overall playability is up to standard now, the feel is superb and the customer should be happy.

To finalise the intonation before double-checking the pickup heights, the guitar is plugged into the Peterson Strobe tuner and the amp. Playing the open E string and getting that to pitch as well as possible – the better the open note, the more accurate the intonation will be – the string is then fretted at the 12th. The strobe tuner shows that both the open and fretted octave are the same. The same process is carried out with all the strings, with only the G and B strings needing to be lengthened a little, as they are very slightly sharp at the octave. Usually, once all the setup points are accurate, the intonation will not be widely out and only some minor adjustments will be required. Whilst the guitar is plugged into the amp, the volume and tone pots can be wound down and back up to make sure the switch cleaning has done the trick and stopped any crackles.

Before having a proper play of the guitar, the pickup heights should be given a final check. Fretting the Bass E at the 21st fret and measuring up from the pole piece on the bass side indicates a perfect ³⁄₃₂in. On the treble side, the measurement is ⅟₃₂in, which is what the factory specs suggest for the pickup height. The middle pickup is slightly lower on the treble side and the bridge pickup is a touch low on the bass side, so these are raised a small amount using a screwdriver. As this guitar is all stock and original, working to factory specs for the pickup heights should be fine. Playing some chords and working the 5-way switch to go from neck pickup to middle pickup and on to the bridge pickup, the tonal range is great and there is no sudden volume change. This is noticeable not just between each pickup but also between bass and treble, which makes this guitar sound great. Positions 2 and 4 have a nice twang to them too.

With the setup complete, any fingerprints are wiped off, the tuning is triple-checked, and the guitar is returned to its case ready to be handed over to the customer. It looks and plays great!

PART THREE

Guitar Repair

CHAPTER 13

Basics

Discussions among the students on setup courses often stray into the territory of repair. Clearly, a huge amount can be rectified, improved and fixed on a guitar with a good setup, but sometimes it is not possible to set the instrument really well without some alteration and/or a repair. Areas that go beyond setup alone are nuts, replacement of parts, and fixing electrical issues outside of the standard dirty pots, although all these jobs are often combined with and added to a setup charge. One key area where a definitive line is drawn is in frets and fret wear. If the setup of the guitar is compromised due to fret wear, it is time to go beyond simple setup and level and re-crown the frets. This very important job is known as fret dressing (*see* Chapter 17). Once the frets have been dressed a few times, it may not be possible to get another fret dress out of them, in which case a re-fret would be needed.

The repair bench

One important practical factor when looking at installing a repair workbench is height. Working over the top of a guitar all day can take its toll on your back so there is definitely an optimum height for the repair bench, which obviously changes a little depending on your own height. A bench top that is 100cm off the ground is much better to work on than one that is lower. Taking my influence from the Galloup School of Lutherie, I work on a bench that is free-standing rather than being built against a wall, so that I can walk all the way around it. Again, taking my lead from Bryan Galloup, all the tools are either in cabinets or within the bench, as opposed to being fixed or hung on a wall above the bench, to avoid them falling and landing on a customer's guitar.

It is important always to be mindful of where tools are on the bench too. Accidentally resting a guitar on a screwdriver or even just a screw will probably cause damage to the lacquer, and it is more than likely that the customer will not give you any repeat work. This can be the difference between survival and failure in the repair business. My main repair bench has four deep drawers that contain all the tools

The main repair workbench.

for setup, fret work, repair finishing and electrics. There is a nice-sized space for the guitar to be placed on a mat and neck stand, as well as some space to the right for the Peterson Strobe tuner and some cleaning products. Nothing can fall on the guitar and being able to have the guitar's headstock over the end of the bench can be helpful, as is being able to walk around

A Squier Strat ready for setting up.

when working on the cherished instruments of other people. I can recall only two examples of an accidental issue that should have been avoided, both of which were due to trying to work too quickly and rushing. Both were easily sorted with some fine sanding, and both times I was honest with the customer and told them that a small problem had occurred and that it had been put right. On a couple of occasions, customers have queried a ding or scratch that they had not noticed before handing it over, which can be tricky, especially if the guitar has not been well looked at before any work began. Knowing that there are standard requirements around the bench and that I can therefore be confident that no additional marks have been made is usually reassuring for the customer. For some guitars, it is recommended that you photograph the instrument from all angles in order to create a record of its current condition. Many guitars from the 1950s – particularly examples of the two main brands, Gibson and Fender – are very

the bench and look at and work on opposite sides of the guitar.

Good lighting is very important too. 'Happy' lights, or full-spectrum daylight bulbs, provide a very clear light that is not only great for the eyes and for taking decent photographs, but also beneficial for mental health. Being inside a repair shop all day without much natural daylight can be a bit demoralising. In my workshop, every light in the ceilings and all the bench lamps are fitted out with full-spectrum bulbs – there must be about 50 in the building!

Whenever an issue happens on the bench, it is important always to be open about it. A high level of professionalism must be the backbone of repair, especially

The main repair room, with all the student benches.

It is helpful to have more than one surface area available for repair, so that the various jobs may be spread out.

The repair racks, clamps, drills and soldering irons.

valuable now, so having a good photographic account of the instrument can be important. More often than not, those 1950s Les Pauls and Strats have seen a lot of action and are hardly in mint condition. Whenever possible and with the customer present, it is always worth looking around the guitar and pointing out any major knocks or defects. Sometimes, the owner may be unaware of some of the marks and the process can be helpful and reassuring.

When working on your own guitar, it is vital to maintain the same high level of discipline. It does make for a better job. Damaging or dinging someone else's guitar may be costly, and doing it to your own will be painful in a different way.

Tools

Going further into lutherie beyond setup, the tools that you will need become increasingly expensive. On average, the cost of tooling up well for setting up guitars will be about £100 and a notched straight edge would take up about 50% of that budget. Some precision screwdrivers, a selection of Allen keys and feeler gauges, and a handful of nut wrenches, as well as a decent 6in steel rule, will be all you will need to get a guitar fully set up. If you add some maintenance products, you will be able to cover both setting up and servicing. Moving into working on nuts requires many different nut files and good-quality ones can be quite costly. Needle files will get you out of trouble on some occasions and are often great for basses, but if you are planning to do repair for a living, a good set of nut files is a must. Anything to do with frets is even more expensive – probably necessarily so. The tools required for fret dressing will start at around £200+ and those for re-fretting will be even more (*see* Chapter 18).

When stocking up on tools, it is always worth buying the best you can afford. Having to replace cheap tools when they break or wear out will cost more money in the long run. Cheaper tools can bend, tend to be less accurate, and often fail to deliver to a high enough standard, inevitably demanding more time and causing more expense as jobs need to be repeated. Specialist tool suppliers such as StewMac in the USA and LMI in Canada can give useful advice, and some years ago they were the only source for good tools. Today, however, there are many more places to buy them.

Sometimes, it is not possible to get hold of a specific tool and making one from scratch, or working another to get it to do a particular task, is all part of being a decent repairer. I did not have any specific woodworking or handcrafting skills prior to taking up lutherie, and making tools was not the first thing to come to mind when I started in the profession. However, there have been many times when it has been necessary to make a bespoke jig or some other item that is just right for the job. Indeed, some specialist lutherie tools are exactly that: work-arounds to get the job done.

Repair or replace?

When a customer believes that their guitar has an issue with some hardware or part, it is always worthwhile checking the setup points as well as being thorough with all the maintenance points before rushing to replace anything. Hardware can of course deteriorate and fail, and in some cases replacement will be necessary, but sometimes cleaning or repairing can resolve it. Many apparent issues with nuts, for example, can be the result of dirty strings, or dirty nut slots that cause the strings to stick or fail to intonate well. The first action should be to clean them up, to see if that helps. They also repair well, especially if they are made of bone. The majority of nuts today are plastic, however, and repairing these can be trickier. In this case, replacing a nut would bring many more benefits than simply enabling it to work again as it should. For more on nuts and replacing them, *see* Chapter 14. Sometimes, especially with some of the lower-end guitars, metal fatigue can be a definite cause of a problem and a reason to replace parts. This is often more viable if the instrument is being well used and enjoyed.

Issues with floating tremolos can often be sorted with a good setup, and the same is true with problematic machine heads. Usually, a guitar that is set up well and properly maintained will perform satisfactorily, but a change of machine heads can improve it a great deal. However, it is not always as simple as swapping one out for another. With short cuts in mass production the replacement parts are not always an exact fit, and this is where a skillful repairer can come into their own. Getting parts to fit well can be a major area of guitar repair and learning how to ream, widen holes and so on, is crucial when carrying out replacements. Sometimes, these are the sort of skills that are learnt on the job.

Nuts

Issues with nuts

It is clear from any setting-up procedure that the nut is a very key part of a guitar. Beyond the various knock-on effects of the setup and the nut height, there are also some common issues with nuts that can be easily sorted, greatly improving the overall function and playability of the guitar. Some of these are factored into a setup, while some go beyond the setting-up process and tip over into repair. It is quite common to have to file the nut gently with some 320-grit sandpaper folded in half, to clean any debris out of the slot. Sometimes, when the string gauge feels slightly tight in the nut – quite common with some of the lower-end guitars that tend to be made for beginners – it will be because the slots have been cut for a 9-gauge string. Going up to 10-gauge or higher, the string can bite and 'ping' in the nut. Another potential issue occurs when there is any sharpness to the side or top of the nut. It may be a minor defect but, once the customer feels it, there is no going

Using a 0.020in feeler gauge to assess whether any one string is high or low.

OPPOSITE: Nut tools.

back. Fortunately, it can be easily sorted by rounding over any sharp or rough edges with a sanding stick with some 320-grit sandpaper on it.

Issues with nut to 1st fret height that are not related to the neck relief or general setup also need to be addressed. Using the feeler gauges under the string and over the 1st fret, putting some radius into the feeler gauge, can highlight one of two things: the height on any one string is either too much or too little. Playing the guitar should highlight both. A string that is high in the nut will feel out of step with the others and will definitely lead off sharp over the first couple of frets, as you are having to press down further to reach the fret. If the string is too low in the nut, there could be some open-string buzz or overtones off the 1st fret. The first issue of the string being too high is likely to be down to a manufacturing issue or a change of string gauge, causing the string to sit higher in the nut. This can be assessed with the feeler gauges placed under the string and over the first fret, which will indicate how much higher one string is compared with the others.

To resolve this, the correct feeler gauge can be placed under the string and the nut slot filed down so that the string touches the gauge. This should bring it to the correct height in relation to the rest of the strings or as per the setup points.

When the nut slot is too low, it needs to be packed with some bone dust and superglue. Once the packing has set, it can be gently filed to the correct and corresponding heights of the other strings. This process is relatively straightforward, but it does require some preparation to prevent any glue harming the finish around the nut area. Some plastic nuts do not always bond well with bone dust and glue. In the early days, I did many repairs to nut slots and saw the bone dust and glue build up nicely, only to move cleanly out of the nut slot when the string was brought up to pitch. Slowly layering up the glue and bone dust definitely helps to avoid this.

A nut with a higher B string.

Some gentle filing with 320-grit sandpaper eases the slot down to the correct height.

Filing down a nut slot with a nut file.

The break angle is very important for a clean-sounding nut slot.

Repairing nuts

Reducing the height of a nut

A Telecaster with some strings that are sitting a little high in the nut, causing some intonation issues, is a good example of how repairing nuts can help. The neck relief and action height are great, but the replaced bone nut just needs a little filing to improve the height and playability over the nut as well as bring the intonation into tolerance around the open-chord positions. Using the 0.020in feeler gauge under the string and over the top of the fret, as well as mirroring the radius of the fret,

it is clear to see that the G and B strings are high, possibly by about 0.004in. Any string leading off the nut and over 0.020in will usually lead off sharp over the first few frets.

To sort this out, the corresponding nut file is used in the slot at a perfect 90-degree angle to the nut, filing with a gentle back angle that follows the line of the string. As a result, the string will lead out of the leading edge of the nut. Filing straight without this angle would allow the string to vibrate in the nut slot and essentially move the intonation line of the leading edge back, causing the string to go even sharper. This may also be heard as an overtone. A string vibrating in the

middle or just off the leading edge of the nut can make the guitar sound rather like a sitar – a sympathetic overtone but not caused by sympathetic strings!

With the two angles considered, the height of the nut is reduced by gently filing backwards and forwards. No particular pressure is needed – less is more in this case – and the thumb of the left hand (if filing with the right) can be used to support a nice steady action. Going into the nut slot straight but coming out at a slight angle can cause the 'V' channel of the nut slot to be a 'W', and a 'ping' will be heard in the nut when the string is bent over it. This is because there is one file line going in and a different one coming out.

This is most noticeable on the High B and E strings and in more severe cases it will occur even further up the fretboard. The issue can be resolved by using a slightly wider file to clean up the bottom of the 'W' channel into a 'V' in that nut slot. When filed slowly and with a straight and steady action, the nut slot will easily reduce in height to the desired amount. When the nut slot difference is, say, less than 0.002in then using a folded piece of 320-grit sandpaper will bring the nut slot in too.

The same results can be achieved by using needle files, which are usually readily available and not expensive. A decent set of needle files can certainly help out with basses. Now, with the nut slots of the G and B string meeting the 0.020in feeler gauge well, possibly slightly lower, not only is the intonation better over the first few frets but there is also a much nicer radius to the strings around this open-chord position, and a proportional string height.

Re-building nut slots

If any slots on a nut need re-building, this can be done using some bone dust and superglue. Low nut slots on a Stratocaster-style guitar can be due to extensive play and tremolo use, which cause the strings to glide in the nut, slowly filing it, especially with the wound strings. The strings are not very abrasive, but they can score the nut over time. This is less likely to be an issue with the unwound strings, although those nuts can become slightly low too. Doing a bone dust and glue repair on the three wound strings should be enough for the nut to carry on performing as it should. When all the other setup points, neck relief and action heights are good, putting some relief into the neck is not always going to help

(with more relief, the nut to 1st fret will be higher). Instead, it would only compromise the current setup, which should always be a qualifier.

Slackening the strings off a little and placing them over the side of the nut – the three wound strings over to the bass side and the three treble strings off to the treble side – enables you to prep the board and the area behind the nut. Both sides of the nut should be protected with some masking tape, to prevent any excess glue going on the lacquer or the fretboard. The bone dust is produced by slowly sanding a piece of bone (most commonly a nut that has been removed and replaced) against a sanding stick with some 320-grit sandpaper on it, and collecting the dust on a radius gauge or a flat block of wood. A fair amount is needed to build up the repair, so it is worth doing more than you think might be required. The superglue needs to be not too fine and not too heavy – Satellite City Green and Gorilla Super Glue both have a good consistency. Put a small amount of glue on either a micro-chisel or a small flat-head screwdriver and then transfer some of it to the bottom of the nut slot. Next, pick up some bone dust on a small tool of choice and gently tap it so the dust falls into and on to the glue in the slot. It should harden quite quickly. Repeat the process, building the glue and bone dust up until the level has clearly risen. This should be enough to raise the string height as needed. If in any doubt, it is always best to repeat the process and file down to the desired nut to 1st fret height after the glue has fully hardened. Although these types of glue do not take very long to go off, an accelerator can be used to speed up the process.

Once the insert of glue and bone dust has set, the strings are returned to the slots and slowly brought back up to pitch. It

should be evident now how much higher the wound strings are sitting in the nut slots that have been filled. It is important to return the strings back to pitch to re-establish the neck relief, which was correct beforehand. The measurement of the nut to 1st fret can also be filed to accuracy. With the feeler gauges underneath the wound strings coming in from the bass side, the distance from the top of the fret to the underside of the string is now closer to 0.030in on all three strings. These will now require some gentle filing down to achieve the optimum string height.

Starting with the Bass E string, it is slackened off a couple of turns, enough to be able to remove it from the nut and place it just outside of the nut slot. A nut file that is slightly wider than the one that corresponds to the gauge of string – so, for the Bass E string, this means a 0.050in file – is used gently and carefully to file following the angle of the string behind the nut. The aim is to have a nice angle and to have the string leading out of the nut at the very front edge, the leading edge. This is where the intonation starts, so, the better the leading edge and launch out of the nut, the better the toleration of the inherent intonation flaws.

If only the back angle is worked, the height will seem not to come down, so the filing angle needs to be reduced a little. On the build courses, students are often very wary of reducing the leading edge too much and tend to focus solely on the break angle. They then become frustrated when they see that the nut to 1st fret height is not reducing in line with the amount of work being put in! They do need to focus on the break angle but also keep in mind that the angle has to reduce the height too. On a six-inline headstock, the E and A strings in particular have quite an angle behind the nut, especially with a good amount of wrap around the tuning post. In this case, being considerate of the break angle while reducing the angle of the nut file so that the height to the 1st fret is lowered will be less of a problem than with the D and G strings, for example.

Working the Bass E string, a few good files with the nut file and a couple of checks to see where the E string is landing in the nut will soon get it to the desired height of 0.020in from the top of the fret to the underside of the string. The process needs to be repeated in the same way for the other two wound strings, taking care that the feeler gauge under the string and over the fret has some radius put into it, otherwise the A and D strings may be filed slightly low. Using the thumb and forefinger to put a little pressure on either side of the feeler gauge around the neck while holding the gauge over the fret will help you to judge how far you need to file. It may be more sensible to get the nut slot filed close to where it needs to be and then finish off with some 320-grit folded sanded paper for the last 0.002in/0.001in.

Care must be taken not to file too vigorously, which usually only happens when you are rushing. Slowing down really helps. There is also a risk of the file falling out of the nut slot and landing on the fretboard, particularly when the file is biting in the slot. If this is happening, a slightly wider file can be used to open the top of the slot a little, allowing the right file to be inserted deeper inside the slot.

Replacing a nut

Repairing a nut is a good and cost-effective way of getting a guitar to play out well and of turning a good setup into a very good setup within a short timeframe. Like many other items on the guitar, nuts are susceptible to wear. Restoring them is very fulfilling, but sometimes they are so cracked, chipped or worn out that they may be beyond repair and need replacing. A nut may be irreparable because it is way too low to fill or because it has had unsuccessful work done on it before. It is quite common for a nut to crack and in this case the best procedure is to remove and replace it. If the nut is plastic, replacing it with bone will bring about an improvement tonally; the natural, denser material allows the note to travel faster, creating a better and more resonant open string. Corian is a man-made form of bone that works well and feels similar to work on. Graphtech nuts are very good too, smooth for the strings and as tonal. Over 90 per cent of my replacement and repair nut work is done using bone, while all of the repairs, the guitars created on the build courses and the hand-built guitars are made with bone nuts. It is a great material.

Removing the damaged nut

Most manufacturers glue the nuts into the slot. There should be only a very small amount of glue – just enough to hold the nut in place during a string change, and so on – but most mass-manufactured guitars are not built by luthiers but by hard-working people in factories. Often, there is an excessive amount of glue, and this can certainly cause problems when trying to remove the nut. Another factor to consider is that quite a lot of mass-manufactured nuts have lacquer over them, which will crack and cause issues around the nut slot area if it is not scored first. This can be done with a brand-new fresh blade, trimmed back to give the sharpest cutting edge, carefully scoring down either side of the bass side of the nut as well the underside of the nut, and then repeating on the treble side. This means that, when the nut is removed, the lacquer should be nice and neat and without any tearing out. On Gibson styles, it is often noticeable when the nut has been replaced because of the missing lacquer around the nut area, especially if it has chipped off lower than the nut. Unfortunately, sometimes this cannot be avoided, even when great care has been taken with the scoring. Using the freshest of blades will reduce the risk, though.

In theory, as long as there is only a tiny amount of glue holding the nut in you should be able to tap its back edge with a sanding stick and a fretting hammer and then gently tap its front leading edge. This should be enough to crack the glue bond underneath the nut and release it from the slot. It may take a few goes but, once the glue bond is broken, the nut will move ever so slightly in the nut slot and will be easy to remove. Another option is to tap it from both back and leading edges and then from the treble side with a small sanding stick and towards the bass side. If it still has not come loose, a micro-chisel can be used, although that can create a little crack on the side of the nut and then send the chisel down into the slot. Once the chisel is underneath the nut and not at risk of marking the slot, it should be possible to lever the nut up and out.

The nut may need quite a lot of tapping and force to get it to free. This can be the case with both Fender-style and Gibson-style necks and nuts. When it has been over-glued, the nut on a Gibson guitar can be even harder to remove, as the glue can seep in between the nut and the edge of the fretboard. Sometimes, even after tapping from the back and front edge, the glue bond will refuse to budge and the top of the nut will come off, leaving the rest of the nut in the slot. This will be frustrating, but it is fixable, if a little time-consuming! The remaining part of the nut needs to be sawn out or chiselled out with a micro-chisel. This can usually be done successfully, removing all the nut and avoiding any other damage.

Glue does not contribute to the tonal character or functionality of the guitar. It is there simply to stop the nut falling out when the strings are being changed. When making a replacement nut from scratch, it can be designed to fit so tightly that no glue will be needed.

With the nut removed, any glue residue or remaining pieces of nut need to be cleaned out of the slot. A good nut seating file, a small flat file with a safe edge or a small micro-chisel can be used for this.

Working with nut blanks

Most lutherie suppliers supply nut blanks, some of which are very close to the size required for the slot. Fender-style blanks made of bone, for example, will measure around 0.140in and the nut width needs to be around 0.125in. The thickness of the bone blank can be taken down by gently sanding against a hard flat surface with some fine sandpaper on it. This will remove the excess quite easily and quickly. Using a belt sander will be even quicker. It is a good idea to measure the inside of the nut slot with the dial caliper ends at the bass, middle and treble side and then test the bone blank thickness after some sanding until the thickness is the same. The Gibson-style blanks

are usually around 0.200in or 0.240in and require a similar amount of sanding initially to just fit in the nut slot. On both styles of guitar, the replacement nuts will be wider than the slot, which will require some filing to get the nut sitting perfectly. Having one side of the blank nut fitting flush – usually to the treble side – and the overhang on the other (bass) side will help with fitting and positioning. When you are putting the nut back in the slot, you just have to get it flush to that treble side to get it positioned correctly to the string spacing you have created. Using a sharp pencil to mark the edge of the fretboard, the slight overhang can be sanded down with either a smooth file or a sanding stick with some 320-grit sandpaper.

On some vintage radius fretboards, the nut slot is also radiused to match. In this case, before you can get the nut fitting and flush to one side, you need to radius the underside of the nut. Some suppliers can supply a curved radiused blank, which can save time, especially for someone who does not have access to the more sophisticated machinery.

To get a bone blank radiused correctly to meet the nut slot, a radius gauge (these are usually 7.25in) is placed carefully on the nut and the radius is drawn on with a pencil. The excess under the pencil line is then sanded off using a small spindle or bobbin sander, or some sandpaper wrapped around a dowel of some sort, to create a nice round edge. The job is much easier with the spindle sander, with the nut flat on the plate and moving the blank up and down slowly, removing the bone from the middle out. Done like this, it will be square to the slot and fit well.

Once the nut is fitting well in the nut slot and flush to one side, a pencil line on the leading edge of the nut can be made

to transpose the radius of the fretboard on to it. This will also act as a reminder that the nut fits best that way, which is a great help when taking the nut in and out during sanding, checking and double-checking. Marking the overhang on the bass side with the pencil also shows how much of that width needs to come off. Now is a good time to do that. The belt and disc sander will make light work of sanding to the line. Without a disc sander it can be done on the side of the bench with a good file, always keeping square to the side and slowly reducing the width.

When the nut blank is ready to check in the nut slot, both sides need to be perfectly flush. You can assess how well it fits and feels by placing your thumb and forefinger underneath the nut, touching the back of the neck, and then pulling the thumb and finger up. If you can feel the nut, it is too wide. Being able to move the nut left or right, to the bass or treble side, within the slot can help with getting the last bit of filing right. Using a sanding stick with some 320-grit sandpaper, gently sand the sides and with the slightest of angles roll down the base of the nut edge to achieve the flush fit that is required. It is worth taking time to get the nut really nicely seated and ensuring that all the corners are fitting tightly, with no gaps.

Positioning the strings

Traditional method

Once the bone blank is fitting well, it is time to determine the string spacing. There are a couple of ways of doing this. The more traditional method is to place the two outer E strings where they sit at least 0.050in inside of the bevel edge as well as taper well down the neck, both outer E strings looking consistent, neither string getting closer or further away to the beveled edge all the way down the fretboard. If the strings sit closer than 0.050in to the bevelled edge, the fretted string is more likely to fall off the fretboard. The rule of thumb and measurement being no less than 0.050in from the beveled edge is also visually noticeable. When checking and trying to get the two outer E strings correct you can easily see when it is not quite right, so trust your judgement by eye; it is often surprising just how exactly we can see the strings' spacing and even more so once we introduce the other strings.

With the two outer E strings positioned, make a pencil mark on either side of each string. Holding the string down behind the nut will stop the strings moving around and allow the line to be drawn accurately. After marking the two outer strings, bring the other strings on to the bone blank and position them, initially by eye. It should be clear when the strings are positioned well, but there is a simple piece of maths to get the spacing correct. Using dial calipers, measure between the centre of the two outer E strings and divide the distance by 5. That will produce the measurement required between each string, although it will need to be confirmed with some visual checking and positioning.

With all the strings in place, the spacing can be checked visually by standing the guitar on the bench and looking down the fretboard from arm's reach. If the dot inlays and/or the pole pieces all line up well, that points to good string spacing – on the assumption that the reference points are also positioned correctly! Once you are happy with the string spacing, mark either side of each

string with a pencil, taking care not to move them.

Now that all the strings are well spaced and the pencil marks have been made, the top of the nut can be scored with a closely matched nut file for each string. The notch in the nut needs to be accurately placed in the middle between the two pencil lines and as close to 90 degrees as possible. Any angle over the top of the nut and between the lines will send the string to the left or right of the desired position. Guide the file with your thumb and make sure you have a good position on the bench so that you can see directly over the top of where you are filing. At this point, the objective is simply to score the top of the nut and make a notch in the correct position to enable you to do a visual check of the spacing. It is not about filing or cutting the nut just yet. With all six strings notched, hold the guitar up on the bench and look at the space between each string. Any discrepancy should be visible.

With all six strings correctly placed, each individual nut can be filed in that exact position. Using corresponding nut files and always working the back file at the same time, the nut to 1st fret height can be reduced. As the slot is filed, use a feeler gauge of 0.020in as a starting point. Filing the Bass E string in close to the desired nut to 1st fret height really helps to provide a visual reference for the next string; this applies to all the strings going across the nut. Using a feeler gauge and making sure the radius of the fretboard is mirrored in the filing of the nut, all six strings need filing down. Often, coming back and reviewing the first outer E wound string shows that it could sit better in the nut and closer to the desired height. Rather than aiming for the precise measurement with the

first filing of the slot, it is more practical to get close and then go back and bring the measurement in, usually with just a tiny amount of extra filing being required. This approach should reduce the number of times when you accidentally cut a nut slightly too low.

Using the string spacing rule

The second method for the positioning of the strings over the nut blank, which is extremely efficient, uses the StewMac String Spacing Rule. Essentially, once the outer E strings are correctly positioned in the traditional way, the rule can be used to map out the other strings. With the spacing rule placed under the strings, the point where the two outer E strings that have been positioned meet with the rule is located with a notch in the rule. A larger notch indicates where the next string would be.

It can take a few attempts to locate all the strings. Quite commonly, when students start to map out their bone nut, they find the two outer Es easily but can only

String spacing rule.

Getting the outer E strings marked.

All the strings are marked on either side with a pencil line.

locate five strings on the rule. It is worth double-checking that all six strings are mapped out once the two outer E strings have been located. A pencil mark on the string spacing rule will help with relocating the place later, or the 'StewMac' wording can be used as reference, if it is in the right spot. This saves time when coming to triple-check the string spacing later on. There are a couple of ways of transposing the spacing on to the nut: either by scoring the top of the nut where the rule and notch shows with a fine nut file, or by marking it with a very sharp pencil.

With all four central strings mapped out, the top of the nut should be notched with the corresponding file, directly on the mark. The strings are then placed in the notches and left to sit there, then checked for correct positioning with the spacing rule underneath the strings and pushed up to the nut. If the rule is pulled up to the underside of the string, it can be easier to see. Ideally, all the strings will be sitting exactly where they should be, although there is still room for minor changes. A string can be 'walked' minutely to the left or right with the file on and in the notch at a slight angle. It is always best to make checks throughout this process, so you do not have to walk the nut slot left or right.

Standing the guitar up on the bench, the spacing can be reviewed by eye, to see if it looks out or not. Students are often surprised by how close they can get to the right string spacing by eye, but they will still need to refer to the string spacing rule to identify any super-fine adjustments that will be necessary before the strings look perfect.

After double- and even triple-checking the spacing, each nut slot can be filed down to the desired height using the corresponding size of nut file and with the feeler gauge over the first fret. As with the traditional method, reducing the height slowly can stop you taking any one slot too low. The radius as well as the gauge of the string should be taken into consideration.

The bone blanks are usually quite a bit taller than required and with a flat-based nut slot rather than a curved one it can

Filing each nut slot.

Reducing the angle helps bring the height in more quickly.

All nut slots are filed close to the desired measurement.

The back file is always worked to get a good break angle off the nut.

Reducing the back file a little to bring the height in.

at 0.030in, it will be easy to score the nut and the point of the pencil will sit in the line. Sanding this amount off on the belt sander will take no time at all. With the nut back on the guitar and the strings placed back in the slots, the amount that needs filing down with the nut files is now greatly reduced and quickly done.

Sometimes, if the bone blank is too tall, having to file deep inside the nut slot can crack the nut, particularly on the outer edges. Be aware that the top of the nut can require sanding down to accommodate the nut file to get lower and lower. Again, with some experience, it is possible for a tech to adjust the nut blank depth a little before any of the spacing has been mapped out.

Finishing off the nut

With all the strings sitting well within the nut and to a desired depth of 0.020in maximum bass side and 0.018in treble side, it is time to reduce the amount of nut that is exposed above the slots. As the strings gradually become thinner, it makes the nut appear as if it is gaining height, so the top of the nut needs sanding down. The corners also need some nice filing, so that they are not noticeable to the touch, say, when a bar chord is fretted around the first fret. Once they have been rounded over, a sanding stick with 320-grit sandpaper will help smooth off the edges, acting a little more gently than the file.

Finishing off the nut carefully will be as important to the customer as the string positioning and heights. It should not be noticeable to the fretting hand around the open-chord positions, and it needs to look great too. Moving up through the grades of sandpaper, a bone nut can also be worked up to a good shine, although

The strings are all deep within the nut.

save time to get the strings spaced correctly, ideally with an even height across them all, and then to take some of the height away by sanding the base of the nut. However, this practice probably requires a degree of experience.

With all the strings spaced correctly and the nut slots notched evenly, the distance from the top of the fret to the underside of the strings needs to be measured accurately with a group of a few feeler gauges. It could be 0.070in at its lowest point. The target for the nut to 1st fret will be 0.020in as a starting point, so at least 0.050in needs to be filed away. Remove the nut, score a line on the bottom at 0.030in and then run a pencil over the scored line. With the dial calipers open and secured

Filing over the nut, to shape it.

Sanding to 320-grit, smoothing out the edges and polishing higher will result in a nice clean-looking nut.

this is not necessary. There have been certain fads and trends over the years in the finishing of replacement nuts; some makers and repairers have preferences as to how much of the string is still exposed, if any at all; some like to have the strings sitting well within the nut and the amount of nut showing above the fretboard looking proportional, not too high. Sometimes, the top of the nut can end up quite low, so that a guitarist bending the B or G strings could pop the string out of the nut, requiring another to be made. It is not common, though, and it can be prevented by favouring a middle ground.

There have also fads been trends with the types of material used over the years. The choice of, for example, plastic or brass for a nut can certainly change the tonal dynamics. This was quite common in the late 1970s and 1980s, perhaps due to the guitars being tonally slightly less bright at the time. Gibsons often had lower-value 300k pots, which tended to 'muddy' the sound. Using a heavier poly-based lacquer on most Fenders at that time may have contributed to the trend too. More recently, graphite has been quite a common request for a nut replacement. Of all the materials, however, bone is the best to work with, and also brings tonal

benefits such as more resonance and a slightly brighter sound.

Making a replacement nut is a great job with so many benefits and if a bone blank is used from start to finish, it creates a part of the guitar that is hand-crafted. Taking some time to finish off the shaping and smoothness of the nut will contribute significantly to the feel and look of the guitar. It is worth spending time to get a nut just right; on some guitars, it may be the only part that has been hand-made, and a pleasing appearance and good functionality will reflect well on the luthier who made it.

CHAPTER 15

Machine Heads

Issues with machine heads

Tuning issues, strings slipping and tuning keys feeling tight or jerky are all adequate reasons for giving some attention to the machine heads. There is not much in this area that can be repaired, and replacement is often the best policy, but it is worth checking a few elements before going ahead. The accuracy and efficiency of the machine heads can be affected by a number of factors: the maintenance and setup of the guitar, the angle of the strings in the nut, the amount of wrap around the tuning post, and the quality of the strings themselves.

There has been a trend to replace machine heads on certain makes and models, swapping them out for locking machine heads. The purpose of this is usually to speed up string changes – the owner only has to thread the string into the tuning-post hole and pull it tight before locking the string in and then bringing up to pitch. This type of machine head can cause some issues, however, particularly when fitted to a headstock without much of a break angle, as might be found on a Telecaster or Strat. Where the break angle is insufficient, the string being locked in without any wrap around the tuning post can lead to open-string buzz. In the late 1970s and 1980s, many Gibson machine heads were replaced by Schaller items, the German brand being favoured over Gibson's own version.

Minor repairs

Replacing the machine heads is often the preference, but some prior minor repair work could help. Many issues with machine heads can be traced back to the setup and general maintenance of the guitar. Even the cheaper machine heads used on some very low-end guitars hold up most of the time. General repairs and improvements to the machine heads can be as simple as screwing in the tuning key buttons if the tuners feel too easy to turn. This should improve the tuning stability. Having the screws that secure the tuner nipped up can help too; any movement in there will have a knock-on effect on the overall tuning. With some open-back tuners, the application of WD40 or a similar lubricant can help them to glide better.

Replacing machine heads

There are a few factors to consider when changing a machine head, including the bushing sizes and the position of any screw holes. An existing hole can be widened with a reamer or mill file. If a hole needs to be reduced in size, this can be done using adaptor bushings or by creating a dowel to fill the hole and then re-drilling for the replacement. The adaptor bushings, particularly when changing from a modern machine head to a vintage-style version on a Fender-style neck, are much better and quicker. With some 3 × 3 machine heads, the screw holes are often at differing angles and this needs to be considered when making a change. Dowelling the small holes where the

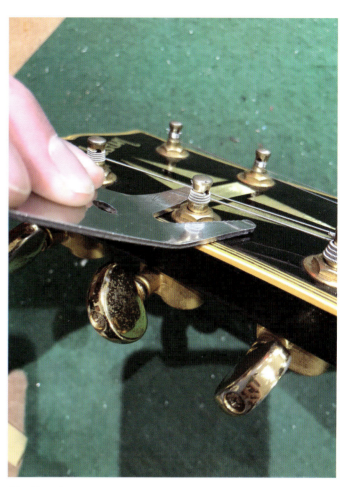

Adjusting the button screws by tightening or loosening can help improve stability.

Checking the bushings are tight.

old machine heads were is relatively straightforward, but the result is often quite noticeable. It is not the easiest of repairs to conceal with either lacquer pens or by spraying the back of the headstock.

One of the most likely repairs is the replacement of the tuners with like for like – a bread-and-butter bench job that avoids all of these issues and which, when combined with a setup, does not take much time on top of the setting-up process.

Another common replacement job is the swapping out of modern machine heads on a Strat-style neck for vintage

items, which will usually require an adaptor bushing. The modern holes are 10mm and the vintage replacements are 8mm, so the adaptor-bushing collar is quite a bit thicker, to hold the vintage tuning post. The bushings and the hole will usually require some work to get a good fit, and the best way to do this – without having to hit them repeatedly with the fretting hammer – is with either a reamer or a mill file. The hole can be gently widened with the mill file, putting pressure into it on the down stroke and moving it around in a circular motion. The first hole always takes a little while, but after filing a few it

becomes easier to see how much work is needed in order to achieve a nice tight push-in fit.

If the machine-head holes are a vintage spec (8mm) and modern machine heads are being fitted, which require a 10mm hole, the holes can be widened either by drilling by hand or on a drill press. It is always wise to go up in small increments with the drill bits – starting with an 8mm drill bit just to be sure and progressing to 8.5mm, 9mm, 9.5mm and finally 10mm. This reduces the risk of sending in a 10mm drill bit that is not perfectly central causing some spacing issues. Doing this with a mill file will take quite some time, and is not

Adaptor bushings to take a vintage-style machine head.

Some gentle reaming is usually required.

recommended due to the amount of wood that needs to be removed from the hole. With the neck off the end of the bench and clamped to the bench, or held in a safe vice, drilling each hole and working up through the drill sizes works well and efficiently.

Very occasionally, the bushings will just drop in the hole, but this means that they might come out. The test is to turn the neck over and give the back of the headstock a tap; if the bushings fall out, then they will need a little glue. It is not advisable to use superglue, as any excess or seepage can be difficult

to remove from nearly all lacquers. It would also make the removal of the bushing trickier than it should be. A small amount of wood glue (Titebond Original is highly recommended) around the bushings and then in the holes will hold them firmly once it has bonded. Any excess can be wiped off before it has dried, or even after. Using Titebond, the bushings should tap out quite easily if necessary at a later date, without any risk of tear-out or upsetting the lacquer on the headstock. The glue takes half an hour to go off well.

To make lining up the vintage-style machine heads a little easier, put some masking tape on a 6in steel rule and butt the rules up to the base of the machine head. The tape is not to secure them in position but rather to act as an extra pair of hands. Once they are all lined up, the screw holes need to be drilled. The screws are very small, requiring a 1.5mm or 2mm drill bit. The drill can be depth-gauged with a piece of masking tape, but great care must be taken not to drill right through the headstock. The screw is not much shorter than the thickness of the headstock and drilling

Using a ruler and some masking tape is like having an extra pair of hands.

Vintage machine heads fitted.

by hand can therefore be problematic. The drill can 'pull' you in before you know it, and the more you do the more the masking tape creeps back, so you need to be very attentive. On your own guitar, a hole on the other side of the headstock might not be too distracting, but on a customer's instrument it certainly would be!

If this slip-up does happen, it usually seems to be on the last drill hole (probably down to the masking tape moving). One way of putting it right is to insert a 2mm mother-of-pearl side dot in the hole. This can look quite good, sitting right at the top of the High E string machine head perfectly in line. However, this type of unexpected repair on a customer's guitar may not be appreciated.

CHAPTER 16

Electrics

Issues with electrics

There can be numerous issues with the electrics on all guitars, but regular maintenance of the pots and switch can really help and reduce the need to repair or replace. Intermittent faults as well as grounding issues are common and problematic, but it is important to be aware that these can be influenced by many other factors outside of the actual electrics in the guitar. On numerous occasions, a customer will bring in a guitar that seems to them to have grounding issues. However, the problem is not noticeable at all when it is plugged in at the workshop. Extension leads, jack leads, overhead lights, the general power of a building, and even dimmer switches at home can all cause problems with a guitar's electrics.

Exploring inside the electrics and being familiar with the schematic of the guitar that has issues can help rule out any obvious flaws or breaks in the grounding circuit, as well as any output issues following the live circuit. Checking those wires would be the place to start.

In my experience the electrical issues with guitars are very rarely caused by the pickups. They are very sturdy and tend to break only with some quite severe manoeuvring or when one of the wires is accidentally broken. On some Tele neck pickups, the start and finish wire can be exposed and broken fairly easily but only with some inconsiderate fitting, especially when they are mounted to the scratch plate.

Output issues are frequently related to live-wire circuit problems, a faulty pot or switch, and more often than not a break in the solder joint on the jack socket itself. On many old-school Stratocasters that have come into the workshop, the live and earth wires on the jack sockets have been broken, which can happen when the jack socket comes loose and then spins around until one of the wires comes off. If the guitar has no output, it will be due to a problem with the live wire (which will usually be white); if it is buzzing and stops when touched, it will be the ground wire (black). These issues, whether output or ground, can usually be sorted out with some simple re-soldering, sometimes even without any extra solder, particularly on the jack socket and sometimes on the switch.

Lack of volume control is another common issue that can be resolved with a simple repair. Essentially, the volume is controlled by sending the signal to ground when it is rolled down. To facilitate this, the third tag of the pot needs to be soldered to the outer casing of the pot. If the volume pot is getting quieter when rolling down but is not going back up again when you get past 3 or 4 and down to 0 then the signal is not going to ground fully. Simply heating up the solder joint that is covering the third tag and making the connection to the outer casing of the pot is enough to improve the contact. If not, a little more solder will help.

Another area of the volume control that is easily rectified involves adding a treble bleed. Many customers complain that the roll-down on their volume pot is too sudden – if they roll down from 10 to 5, all the volume disappears, because the curve down to zero is too steep. This can be associated with cheaper pots as well as audio taper, which will sound like the volume goes too quickly. Sometimes, differing values of potentiometers will add to the problem. Using a treble bleed – a low-value capacitor and a resistor soldered between the two tags on the volume, between the input and output – will enable the roll-down to be much more gradual. When the control is rolled down, the volume pot takes out the treble first, so adding the treble bleed circuit to keep the treble in for longer makes it sound like the volume is decreasing much more slowly. It is a simple and cost-effective upgrade that has been added to many customers' guitars in the workshop and a component that is always in our hand-made instruments, to give a nice taper to the volume control.

If the guitar lacks any tone control, this can be due to one of the sides of the capacitors' feet not touching or not being held by a good solder joint. Simply heating up the tag or the base of a pot where the capacitor is held should get the tone back up and running.

Switch issues are also down to solder joints going off or the live wires being pulled. Referencing the schematics for the guitar or a good schematic for that pickup configuration will help locate the issue. If the manufacturer's schematic is not available, the Seymour Duncan's website is a great resource that will produce a schematic for nearly all pickup and control possibilities.

Replacing pots, capacitors, switch and jack sockets

A great way to improve the electrics on many guitars is to replace the pots, capacitor, switches or jack sockets. All these components have occasional faults, and swapping them out can greatly improve the performance and tone of a guitar. Most mass-manufactured guitars have low-quality electrical parts and changing the pots for better-quality items will straight away give better roll-down on both the volume and the tone pots. They will feel better to use, too. Swapping out the capacitors as a standalone job is a great way of improving how well the tone works, as well as the function of the tone pot. Capacitors have differing values, which affect the way they alter the tone when they are rolled down and can really open up new tones to a guitar. Sometimes, though, just changing all the parts out for better-quality items is good enough, rather than exploring differing values of either pot or cap.

The switches used on mass-manufactured guitars can also be improved with better-quality replacements. There will be little change to the functionality of the switch, but the modification is worthwhile as it will give a better feel to the switch and, more importantly, a longer life. The same can be said for the jack sockets. It is quite remarkable just how bad cheap jack sockets are compared with the Switchcraft ones, in terms of the thickness of the metal, the sleeve and general build quality. The replacement items should last a lifetime.

With a solid-body guitar, where the access is through the back, soldering over the guitar and with the components fitted inside is workable but it is slightly more difficult than having the electrics on a plate. It is always worth doing some prep to protect the back of the guitar, just in case of any solder spits. With the electrics all mounted on a scratch plate (Strat-style) or a control plate (Tele-style), it is often necessary to remove all the strings and the plate from the guitar.

On a Stratocaster or any similar guitar where the pickups and all the controls are mounted to a scratch plate, and if all the components are being replaced, it is good practice to have the scratch plate completely removed and parts changed on the bench and with the body and neck out of harm's way. The scratch plate can be hooked up with the jack socket and plugged into an amp to test that everything is functioning properly before re-fitting on the guitar. The jack socket does need unsoldering and then re-soldering back on after, but it is far better to identify a problem with this style of electric configuration prior to fitting it and then re-stringing the guitar. On Telecaster styles, where all the controls are on a plate, the strings do not need to be removed, so they are a lot easier to modify. There is no excuse not to explore some modifications if the electrics do not seem quite right.

When swapping out a switch like for like (albeit a better-manufactured part), the corresponding schematic for the model can be followed. Alternatively, if there is enough room and play on the wires, it can be de-soldered with the replacement very close by and the wires simply transferred – assuming it was correct beforehand! Pre-tinning the switch and its tags where the wires need to be attached is very helpful. With the tags pre-tinned you can come back with the required wire and just heat up the pre-tinned tag and, once it is hot, push the wire through the hot solder and tag. Wait for the solder to cool, without blowing on it, and within a few seconds the solder joint will be solid again, with the hook-up wire firmly in the middle.

Swapping out a capacitor is done in the same way. Heating up the legs will loosen the contact and some tweezers or long-nose pliers can then be used to safely remove the

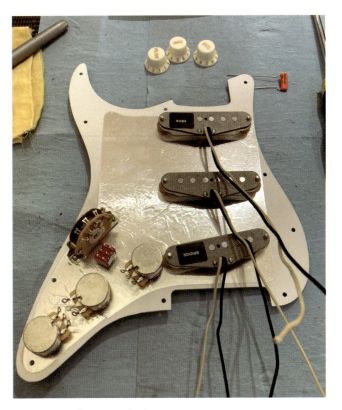

Loading up a Strat scratch plate.

Following the schematic to wire up the pots.

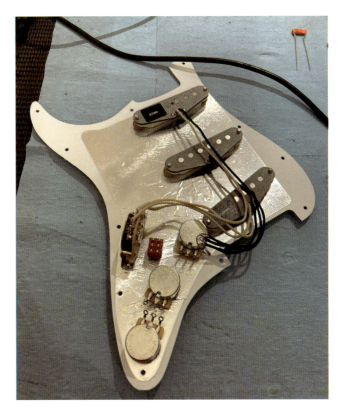

Wiring up the live circuit.

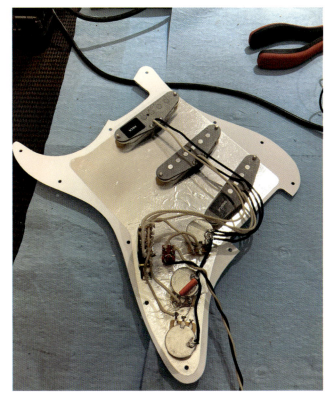

Loaded Strat scratch plate.

Soldering

Changing the pots, capacitor or switch requires some soldering, which is not a difficult task but certainly involves some pitfalls. When I studied in the USA, the first guitar project was a Telecaster, basically building an all-parts body and neck that needed finishing, as well as the neck fretting and all of the assembly, including the electrics. When it came to the day that the control plate was to be fitted out and the electrics wired up, the teacher told us all to go ahead, following the schematic. I had no previous experience with a soldering iron and certainly no experience with wiring up a guitar's electrics. Soldering may have been taught in US schools, but it had not been a subject at mine and no family member had passed on their knowledge to me either. However, by watching some of my colleagues, as well as asking questions, I managed to get the Telecaster wired up and working! The point is that the technique is not over-complicated, but the complete novice will definitely benefit from some helpful tips. People who have more experience will know the nuances of their own soldering irons and may have developed their own way of doing things.

The common ground is heat transference – using the hot solder to transfer the heat is absolutely key, so pre-tinning the tip of the soldering iron is the way to go. Picking up a little solder on the tip and then taking the iron to the appropriate tag, to either heat up a solder joint to remove a wire or to tin the tag that you are wiring up to, the heat will be transferred more quickly, and the job will be much easier than heating up the joint or tag and adding solder. Scoring the back of a new pot is recommended so that the solder has something to key into. With heat transference in mind, heating up the back of a pot takes time. Again, the best way to speed up that process is to add some solder to the tip of the iron and then, once it is sitting on the back of the pot, add more solder to the tip and the back of the pot. This should enable the solder to flow easily and add a nice solder blob to the back of the pot. All ground wires are usually soldered to the back of the volume pot.

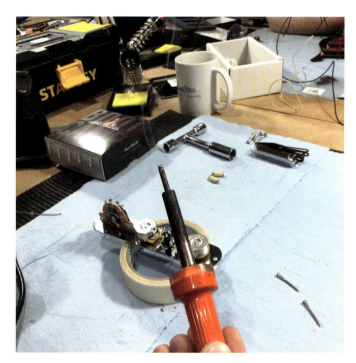

Pre-tinning the tip of the soldering iron.

Pre-tinning the tag on the volume pot.

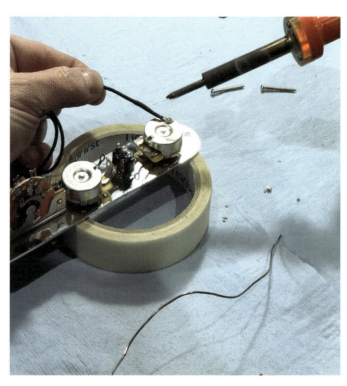

After scoring the back of the pot, a small blob of solder ready for the earth wire.

The solder is re-heated and the earth wire is applied.

cap. Putting an elastic band around the grips of a pair of long-nose pliers effectively gives you an extra pair of hands. This can also come in very handy when replacing the jack socket, to hold the one being replaced while the ground and live wires are disconnected. The pliers can then be used to hold the new jack socket, making light work of getting the live and ground wires back on. If you decide to replace a jack socket for a better one, Switchcraft items are recommended. Note that the tag that says 'Switchcraft' on it is the ground/sleeve, so you need to attach and solder the black wire to it. The other is the live!

Replacing the pickups

Replacing the pickups is a great way to alter the sound and tone of the guitar. Among the many reasons to change them

is the chance to experience some differing tones and dynamics, the desire for a lower or higher output, or simply to have items that are better made than those that are fitted by the mass manufacturers. Apart from just wanting to swap out pickups for an artist-endorsed product or another new boutique brand, it is good to acknowledge the current output and whether the replacements will be hotter, will have more output, or will create a more vintage vibe that has a lower output. An understanding of the magnet that is fuelling the pickups – either those that are on the guitar already or the ones that are going in – can give a much better insight into how the tone will change, and what is being added or taken away. A multi-meter tester can be used to check the outputs of the pickups. Plug a jack lead into the jack socket and then, with the live tag (usually red) of the tester placed or held on the tip of the other end of the jack lead and then the ground tag

(usually black) on the sleeve of the jack lead, you can get a reading. With the tester set to 'ohms' and the volume and tones on full, it is easy to switch between the pickup selections and record the output.

Many mass-manufactured pickups are perfectly fine and do exactly what is asked of them. However, there is a lot to be gained from dialling in a tone from some of the terrific pickup makers that are out there.

There are a couple of different types of wire to bear in mind. With humbuckers, it can be braided and shielded wire, containing the live wire within an outer ground wire. This needs to be cut to expose the inner wax cloth live wire and allow the outer ground wire to be soldered easily, usually to the back of the pot. The other type that can come with a humbucker is a four-core wire, which allows the pickup signal to be split from one coil to another, as well creating phasing. Essentially, being

Testing the output of the pickups using a multi-meter and a guitar jack lead: connecting the red to the tip of the jack and the black to the outer sleeve will show you the output.

A double-humbucker Fender in for a pickup change.

New pickups being loaded in.

two single coils, the humbucker has two starts and finishes, so using four-core wire brings a load of tonal possibilities.

The other traditional type is the vintage waxed-cloth wire, usually white for live and black for ground. The inner core is usually pre-tinned and of a decent thickness. The outer wax shield does not need cutting to expose the inner live wire. Instead, when the wire is being soldered to, say, one of the tags on a switch, the pre-tinned tag can be re-heated, the cloth pulled back and, once it has been sufficiently heated, the wire can be pushed through the solder joint. When the solder has cooled completely and the joint has set, the cloth wire can butt up against the tag, thus insulating and shielding the wire efficiently.

More modern wires may be wrapped in white or black plastic. The downside to this is when this type of wire is exposed to the heat and melts a little, the shielding effect of the outer wire is reduced significantly. The variations in the different types of wires can really improve tone and the overall quality of the output.

Practically, when changing pickups, the strings will need to be removed, as well as the pickups themselves, from either the pickup surrounds or the scratch plate. There are commonly two height-adjustment screws that hold the pickup to the surround or plate, and also secure a spring or rubber grommet. Unscrewing these will remove the pickup from the surround or plate. The live and ground wires are then removed by heating up the solder joint for the live wire, which is usually wired up to the switch, and the ground wire, which is wired to the back of the volume pot. With these two wires de-soldered and the pickups free of the surround or plate, the pickup is clear and can be removed. The new pickup is fitted to the surround or the back of the plate and the live and ground wires are re-attached. With a pair of humbuckers, it is best to load these up to the pickup surrounds and then send the wires through cavities to the control cavity, for wiring up to either the volume controls or the switch.

CHAPTER 17

Fret Dressing

Understanding fret dressing

Fret dressing is the process of levelling the frets in relation to one another and then re-crowning them, bringing them back to where they were when first fitted, but ever so slightly lower. When the frets wear, most noticeably around the open-chord positions, small indents appear, sometimes coupled with some subtle overtones. When they are deeper, this may cause some fret buzz.

Higher up the fretboard, any indents may be less noticeable, but the tops of the frets can look flattened off. This is due to more bending of notes higher up as opposed to around the open-chord position area. A fret dress is usually required when the setting-up process is compromised to the point where it is necessary either to add relief into the neck and or raise the action height to a position that is not acceptable. The process of adding relief or raising the bridge height may allow the strings to clear the fretting issue,

Fret-dressing tools.

Frets can become very worn, especially around the open-chord position.

cents. (Remember, for each cent of a note the string length compensation is 0.010in, so, with a fret that is 0.100in, the middle of the fret is 0.050in. With a very worn indented fret the string could be leading off 0.030in back, or three cents of a note behind where it should be.) Any sharpening like this might not be very noticeable on its own, but the note will often be played along with other notes that are also slightly out due to wear on the frets, but by a different amount. As a result, the intervals will be stretched too, creating an even more imperfect intonation.

With a very worn fret, where the crown is almost flat, not only will the intonation be compromised but also the propensity for fret buzz will be greatly increased. This is because the fretted note is being played on a nearly flat surface. When the note is attacked, the small initial vibration of the string will hit in front of the fretted note on that fret as well as the next fret. This will almost certainly be heard as fret buzz rather than an overtone.

What is nearly always apparent, particularly on customers' guitars that they have learnt on and played almost exclusively, is that there will be some defined indents around the open-chord positions, as well as some wear around the upper middle of the fretboard (the pentatonic area). There will usually be some degree of flattening of the higher register too, most commonly around the 15th to 19th fret area. When a beginner is learning to play the guitar, they often use too much pressure with the fretting hand and, as they are usually playing open chords, this is where the indents begin to appear first. As they progress into bar chords and perhaps some lead playing, the wear becomes more even across the fretboard, but tends to head upwards. As they learn more lead and play scales further up, along with some

but it will always be at the cost of a good setup. Some customers do not like to see indents at all and have the frets lightly dressed at the first sign of them appearing. This is perfectly fine, as the amount of fret being taken off will be very minimal. The opposite of this is a player who leaves the frets for too long, until the indents are so deep that the fret-dressing job is very difficult, or sometimes impossible. At that point, a re-fret will be necessary.

Frets that are all level to one another as well as crowned well will ensure a great setup or an ability to set the guitar up to suit any style. With the frets level and a great launch off the top of the well-crowned frets, the vibrating pattern of the string is accommodated by the setup and the neck relief, and the fretted string clears

the next fret evenly and cleanly. A well-crowned fret will also intonate better than a worn fret. Often, when a customer has concerns about intonation around certain playing positions, this can be down to unevenness and wear on the crown of the fret.

The frets are positioned sitting to the exact measurement of the scale length divided by 17.817. The fret is like a 'T', with a barbed tang in the centre and a semi-circle crown. The intonation line, directly in the centre of the fret, can be seen quite clearly on unbound fretboards. On most Fenders and similar styles of guitar, the lower tang of the fret – where the note intonates from – is clear in the side of the fretboard. If there are any indents in the frets, the string can sit slightly behind the true intonation line, therefore sharpening the note up to a few

big bends, the tops of the frets tend to flatten. When the guitar has its initial fret dress, all of these areas will be levelled and re-crowned and usually the player will be playing much more evenly across the fretboard. As a result, the next stage of wear will be much less noticeable. Hopefully, after a few years the customer will be a super guitar player and may have more than one guitar, and this will be reflected in more even fret wear across the board.

Customers often ask how many fret dresses a guitar can have. The answer obviously depends on the amount of wear and the time between each fret dress – or, indeed, whether it has been done at all. If there is an even amount of wear, it is quite common to be able to fret dress a guitar at least three times. The lower the frets become from repeated levelling the harder it is to re-crown them. There are times when a guitar's originality is more important than how well the frets can be re-crowned in a fret dress. One particular 1960s Gibson ES335 came into the workshop with very low and original frets and a customer who did not want to re-fret the guitar, due to its value with the original frets on. The levelling was fairly straightforward, but the crowning was very tricky. The frets did eventually crown to the centre but it involved finalising the final crown by hand with some 320-grit sandpaper and gently bringing each side of the fret to the centre (*see* below). It certainly is possible to dress frets numerous times and get even the lowest frets playing well, but the execution does become more difficult over time.

Tooling

Like many skilled jobs, this area of work requires the right sort of preparation and some good tools. Tooling up for the job could cost a minimum of £150 up to about £300, depending on the source of the tools. In any area of repair that falls within a specific lutherie skill, the tools are very important, and it is essential to buy the best you can afford. If you are planning to do it for a living, you only want to buy your tools once, rather than trying to save money with cheap alternatives and having to replace the tools when they can no longer do the job effectively or efficiently. The wrong tool will make the job more time-consuming and it will be harder to get the frets back up to a super finish.

StewMac fretting tools are the ones that I have learned with, used, and taught with, and have always been great. Even the crowning file from 2007 is still going strong and is put to good use regularly today.

A fret-levelling bar is used to file the tops of the fret level in relation to one another. This needs to be performed on a straight neck and once all the preparation of the fretboard has been done. They come in two sizes, 16in and 8in. I started out with the 16in bar but, once I started to teach fret dressing, I found the smaller one better for my students. Seeing the tops of the frets losing their ink and the direction of travel, and making corrections along the way, is easier with the 8in bar. It really helps complete novices with fret dressing their guitars.

To re-crown the frets, I have always used a 300-grit diamond fret file. There are 150-grit diamond files, but these are not recommended due to the difficulty of getting the 150-grit marks out of the frets. At 300-grit, the score lines on the frets can easily be worked and polished out in good time. The diamond file is also recommended over a

320-grit adhesive-backed sandpaper is worth the extra cost.

steel fret file, which tends to 'chatter' and again scores the fret a little too much. More importantly, it will fade over time and will need replacing. Once you have acquired the skill of fret dressing, you will find that it is very much a core job for a repair business. With every new customer, there is another potential fret dress in the future, so you need your tools to last.

The last job with a fret dress is to get out of there with nicely polished frets. There are many polishing papers to choose from, including micromesh papers from 1500-grit up to 12,000-grit, which will achieve a great shine on the frets. Microfibre papers can be used in the same way. On the build course, once everyone has levelled and re-crowned, they re-use the same 320-grit sandpaper that they have used for levelling to start removing the worst of the score lines made by the crowning file. Depending on how many passes it has done, the self-adhesive paper sandpaper that has been stuck to the levelling bar will be about 600- to 900-grit, so this is a really good way to start as well as being cost-efficient. Wet and dry high-grit sandpapers – usually 1000-, 2000- and 3000-grit – can also be used. With every fret being polished by every paper, the result will be nice and shiny. Another way of finishing them off cost-effectively is to re-use the same 0000-grade wire wool that you have used to clean the unfinished fretboard and polish up the frets during regular maintenance.

Preparation

Fret dressing requires a good understanding of neck relief and truss-rod adjustment, and this is the first point of preparation. If the frets are to be levelled successfully, the neck must be perfectly straight. When not at tension and without the strings on, most necks will be straight. However, some can have some negative relief, or back bow, and some will have the smallest amount of relief still in the neck. With any negative relief, the truss rod will need a little slackening off, so counter-clockwise, say, from 2 to 12 on the clock face. When the neck still has some relief, the truss rod will need a little tightening, clockwise. All of this needs to be as accurate as possible and ideally measured with a notched straight edge. Good practice would be to record what the relief was in the neck prior to the strings coming off, as well as making a note of how the neck needed to be adjusted prior to fret dressing. The job of fret dressing also includes re-setting up the guitar once everything is level, crowned and re-strung. Having a note on how the neck was adjusted can help get the guitar back to its optimum setup. Naturally, with the frets now slightly lower due to the levelling, the setup will need to be looked at anew, but having notes will help you get to the final points more quickly.

Sometimes it is important and necessary for the neck to be secured during the levelling to ensure that it is straight. This can be done with some straps through the bench and up and over the fretboard retaining the neck and pulling it into zero relief. If the neck has negative relief, some cauls behind the neck can push it up and into zero relief. StewMac have designed a good neck jig that does this very well, although it is pretty expensive. Some workshops have a special fret-dressing table where the neck can be strapped up to secure the correct straightness. In my experience, nearly all necks will get to zero relief – completely straight – either without their strings in tension or with a small amount of truss-rod adjustment. Sometimes, with a neck that has a very small amount of negative relief that will not adjust, the weight of the levelling bar is all it takes. Some experience and a deep understanding of how the neck might move will help here.

Continuing with the preparation, one rule of thumb of fret dressing is that, if the neck can be removed from the body, then it is always best to do this. For any bolt-on style guitar (this would include all Fender styles, as well as many others), the strings are removed and the three or four screws holding the neck in place are carefully un-screwed and removed. Then, with the neck still in place, the guitar is placed carefully back on the bench and a little pressure on the headstock is applied to enable the neck to pop up out of its pocket. The neck and neck pocket are a tight fit to one another, but it should be fairly easy to remove the neck. Angling the neck down and out of the neck pocket will reduce the risk of cracking the lacquer. It is always best to do a visual check of the area around the neck and pocket at this stage. There may already be signs of the neck being removed in the past, such as hairline cracks or some very fine checking. There is no need to score around the area with a blade. When the guitar is made, the body and the neck are finished apart from each other and then fitted, but over time the finish can expand or contract.

With the neck removed, the body can be put to one side, out of harm's way, and the neck is much easier to work with. Sometimes, being able to turn the neck around freely can help get a few frets better crowned. With a glued-in set-neck or neck-through style of guitar, this is not an option. With single-cut body shapes, such as almost all Les Paul styles, it can be quite difficult to work on the higher-register frets – for a start, the selector switch is in the way. There are now special tools to help with this, but it is possible with a standard crowning file, just a touch trickier. Unscrewing the switch back plate on that style and then unscrewing the nut from the three-way toggle switch will cause the switch to fall into the cavity, more out of the way. Turning the whole guitar around on the bench will also make it slightly easier for the upper frets.

With the strings off and the neck separated from the body (or not), the next part of the preparation is to use masking tape to protect the fretboard and leave just the frets exposed. Most fretboards will be fine with masking tape on, but if the fretboard is finished and lacquered, usually a maple fretboard, it is very important to check the state of the finish first. If there are any checking lines in it, masking tape could lift the lacquer off when it is removed, and any chips in the lacquer will almost certainly be pulled off with the removal of tape. If this is the case, the fret dressing will need to be done without masking tape, which will make it trickier. There will also be slightly more risk of putting marks in the lacquer or on the fretboard when re-crowning. Although the crowning file should not be worked on the fretboard, the two can touch. Using low-tack masking tape can help, and the adhesion of normal tape can also be reduced by putting it on your clothing before it goes on to the board.

Pull out about a metre of masking tape, place it lightly on the bench and then cut it clean in half with a blade. Place the masking tape up and on to the fretboard right at the edge of the first fret. It should not touch any part of the fret and at the same time you should not be able to see any of the fretboard. If the masking tape rides up the fret, it will gum up the diamond file and make the crowning that little bit more difficult. Prep one side of each fret, working all the way up the fretboard, with the first bit of tape, then use the other bit of tape to mask up the other side of the fret. This will work pretty much all the way up the fretboard, but when you get to the higher frets you will need to cut the tape in three to have narrower pieces. It is just as important to get the tape perfectly flush to the frets here.

Students of fret dressing often underestimate how important this preparation

Cutting the masking tape to prepare for fret dressing.

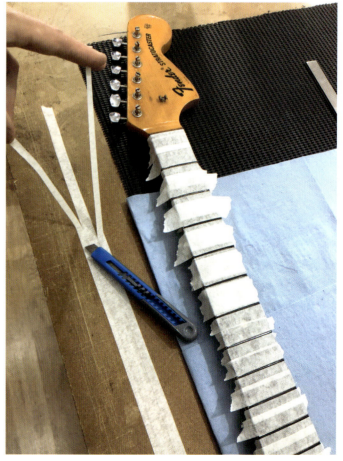

Cutting the masking tape into three for higher up the fretboard.

A masked-up fretboard, with the frets inked up ready for levelling.

possible. The fretboard is prepared carefully with masking tape and the tops of the frets are inked up. It is sometimes advisable to check the neck pickup height or mask over with tape so that the levelling bar does not foul the pole pieces (on a fixed-neck guitar) and maybe also mask over the nut in case the levelling bar is sent too far up the fretboard. Adhesive-backed 320-grit sandpaper is carefully cut around one length of the levelling bar or a strip of sandpaper is stuck on to it using some double-sided tape. The adhesive-backed sandpaper is well worth the extra cost, as it has many uses other than just fret levelling.

Levelling

The aim when levelling the frets is to have no ink left on any one fret from one side of the bevelled fret to the other side of the bevelled fret. The purpose of inking the top of the frets is to indicate how level the frets are in relation to one another once the levelling bar has been used going up and down the fretboard, carefully following the radius of the fretboard. Any remaining ink shows that a fret or a part of the fret is lower than another that has no black ink left on it.

Starting on the bass side of the fretboard and with the levelling bar just slightly over the edge of the frets but not putting any angle into or on to the bevelled edge, proceed up the fretboard – from the 21st or 22nd fret up to the 1st fret – following the line of the Bass E string. Next, come down the fretboard from the 1st fret to the last, down the line of the A string, and continue this up and down following the strings, D, G B and E. Continually heading up and down the board but also along ensures that you are following the radius of the fretboard. Do not

is. Any amount of tape that is on the fret rather than being perfectly flush to it really does make for a messier job and one that is harder to execute. Taking time over preparation at this stage is key. Having the masking tape ends all left up on one side, usually the treble side of the fretboard, enables you to place a piece of masking tape all the way along from around the first fret to the last over these ends, joining them all together, which enables you to remove them much more quickly once you're ready to remove the masking tape. This will stop it getting too stuck to the side of the neck, although handling the neck will inevitably cause that to happen. It is best to avoid having to pick excess tape off the back of the neck with your nails or another tool, as this could harm the finish. With satin-finished necks, it can be even more noticeable if the tape is stubborn to remove.

The final part of the preparation for this job is marking up the tops of the frets with a black marker. The ink needs to be visible from the bevelled edge of the fret bass side to the bevelled edge of the fret treble side. The fret does not need to be completely covered with ink, but there should be a clear, defined line. When the frets are quite worn and flattened off, the ink needs to be the width of the top of the fret. It is best to avoid going over and on to the bevelled edge as this can take extra time to clean off and risks putting black ink on the side of the fretboard. It can all be cleaned off but this will become rather time-consuming. The black line on top of the frets is essential to this job, for both the levelling and the re-crowning.

Levelling and re-crowning

To start fret dressing, the strings need to be removed and the neck relief needs to be at zero. The neck should be removed if introduce a new edge that will be slightly inside the old. If this happens, it can be crowned out and sent back by someone who has some experience, but it is best not to lean the levelling bar over the bevelled edge in the first place.

A balanced, well-weighted and nicely controlled pass should result in the tops of the frets having less ink on them. Frets that are very new will level out very quickly, with maybe just a single fret being exposed as causing an issue due to being too tall. That fret will be more filed and levelled down by the bar than the ones around it. Where one fret might have been causing a similar issue – perhaps a low one in the middle of the fretboard – this will be the one with some ink still on it when all the other frets are clean. If there is still ink on any fret, or any part of any fret, the levelling bar needs to make another pass, starting at the bass-side top of the fretboard to the 1st fret area and back up, following the lines of the strings, until all the black ink is gone.

Any indents that were showing on a fret beforehand will require further levelling. If there is any black ink visible in the indents after a few passes, it is advisable to change over to 600-grit, or maybe higher, and continue to level the frets using the levelling bar. With a fresh piece of sandpaper, the frets should all come down to the lowest point in the indents and the tiny black marks will go. The levelling of the frets will only be complete once there is no ink left on any fret.

Never try to level one troublesome area where black ink is visible on a few frets. Always start at the starting point and work across. Trying to chase out ink from one spot separately will lead to that area being lower than anywhere else. Always level all the frets every time!

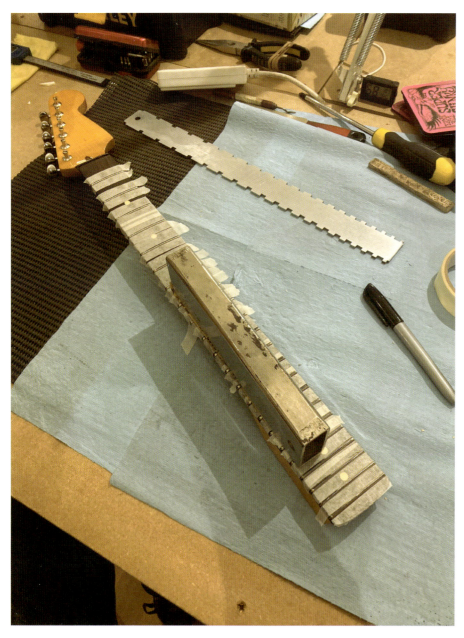

The levelling bar ready for the job.

follow the string lines too literally, though, as this is not how the fretboard is played. Try to be smooth and fluid, crossing the entire tops of the fret from bevelled edge to bevelled edge. Going up the board and then stopping and moving the bar across to come down the next string will not level the fret well. Each pass (from bass side to treble) should be even and flowing. Having

your thumb over the side of the levelling bar when going up the bass side will make you aware of how far the levelling bar is to the side of the frets. When you are travelling down the treble side, the fingers can be used to let you know how much of the bar is leaning over the treble side of the frets. The bar really should not be allowed to come over the bevelled edge as this will

Once the frets have been levelled, there will be no ink remaining on the top of them.

and thinner that line, the better it is in many respects.

The diamond fret file is used from the bass to treble side and starting on one side of the fret, as low as possible, with an angle on it that is gradually reduced, moving closer and closer to 90 degrees. There comes a point where the file starts to connect with the fret and that is when it will start to work and remove the black ink from the sides of the fret first. The other side of the fret is then worked with a similar angle, again reducing it until the file starts to connect with the fret, all the time going from bass side to treble, and following the radius of the fret and fretboard.

To start, aim for a nice consistent black line on top of the fret and try to file an even amount off each side so that the line is central. At this point, the file needs to be angling and moving toward 90 degrees, making the line on top of the fret thinner. Working each side brings the line narrower and narrower, making the crown of the fret. If small triangles start to appear at the end of the frets or just on one side, the file needs to follow the radius better. The triangles of black ink mean that the file has not gone over the end of the fret but has cleared it. They need to be reduced, especially on a Strat-style guitar, where the outer strings are often quite close to the bevelled edge.

The lines on each fret should be consistent with one another and as fine as they can be. When I was studying in the USA, every time I thought my lines were fine enough, the teacher would come around and tell me to keep going. It became a bit of a joke and I say the same to my students today. If the line on the top of the fret was paper thin, it would be around 0.003in, which in lutherie is quite a lot! A hair can

Re-crowning

With all the frets level in relation to one another, it is time to ink up the tops of the frets again. This time it will be very noticeable that the frets are now flat and the score lines on top of the frets will give some resistance to the marker pen. Always ink up the tops of the frets from bevelled edge to bevelled edge.

The aim of re-crowning the frets is to bring them back to a nice round and even shape with the smallest of black lines – hairlines – on the top of the fret. This black line proves that all the frets are level to one another, as it was put on after the levelling process. The finer

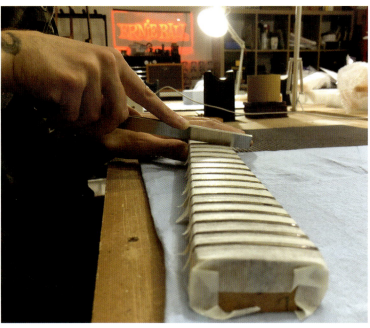

Re-crowning the frets, making the black line as narrow and as faint as possible.

Crowning the frets, following the radius.

Crowning the frets, making the line increasingly faint and narrow.

Keeping going, until the black ink line is as narrow as it can be.

The first few frets are beginning to look good, but the line still needs to be narrower.

be measured at about 0.001in – this tiny width would be ideal for every fret, if it was possible.

The reason why the black line on the top of the fret needs to be so fine is because this will help all the strings to fret as well as they can on the centre – the middle of each fret is the true intonation line. If all the frets are in this state, the intervals should all be consistent and provide the best opportunity for equal temperament. It is always worth aiming for perfection, even though a fretted instrument can never be perfect!

There is also a practical reason for getting the black line super-fine and that is because it makes the polishing-out easier. Where the line is inconsistent or slightly too wide, and where ink remains on the flat part of the fret, this will be visible in some lights to the naked eye, as well as being noticeable when the guitar is played. If a scratchy area is noticeable on a fret or even a few frets, especially when bending a note, it means that the fret is still flat and either needs better crowning or polishing out.

Once all the black lines on top of the frets are as fine as they can be, it is time for polishing. Essentially, this involves working through a range of sandpapers, getting finer and finer, to remove the score lines until the frets become super shiny again. To start with, the grit of the sandpaper must be close to that of the crowning file; so, with a 300-grit diamond file, the first paper should be 320-grit, or slightly finer. The worn strip of 320-grit paper from the levelling bar would probably be at around 600-grit after a few passes, so this would be a a good place to start. Taken off the bar, cut in half and folded over, it will be ideal for tucking in behind one side of the fret and then sanding bass to treble side while also moving up and gently over the top of the fret coming down the other side. This should remove all the black ink and the fine line on top of the fret. If some ink and line remain on that fret, the process should be repeated before moving on to

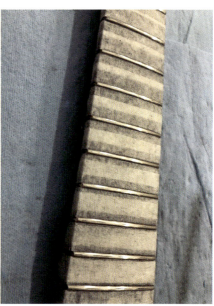
Very faint lines across the frets.

the next fret. When first going over the top of the fret with the polishing paper, it is important to be gentle. It should not require a great deal of pressure. If it does, then the line is possibly too wide and more work with the diamond file is needed.

Once all the frets are fully clean of ink, they may look quite dull, but the important point at this stage is to have them all very consistent. Increasingly fine papers, either micromesh or microfibre, are then used, always starting at and tucking into the bottom of the fret and moving from bass to treble side, going up the side of the fret, over the top and then down the other side. With the polishing papers becoming finer and finer, the frets will become shinier and shinier, losing all the score lines and marks from the diamond fret file. It is not entirely necessary to go all the way up to 12,000-grit – 1500-grit will produce frets that look and feel absolutely fine – but a little extra effort will give a really full shine.

After polishing, the masking tape can be carefully removed. If the fretboard is unfinished, it is not necessary to be too careful, but with a finished fretboard it is always best to be very gentle so as not to disrupt the finish. With the tape removed, the fretboard is cleaned to remove any residue from the masking tape. An unfinished fretboard, perhaps made of rosewood or ebony, can be cleaned with some 0000-grade wire wool and wood oil soap. Pump polish can then be applied to the back of the neck to clean up any residue from the tape. For a finished fretboard (most commonly maple), a good guitar pump polish can be used quite liberally to clean off anything left behind by the masking tape, as well as around the back of the neck where the tape has sat. If the frets dull slightly at this point, placing the fret guard over them and using a fresh piece of 0000-grade wire wool will bring back the shine very quickly for both styles of fretboard. On an unfinished fretboard, going back over the frets with the 0000-grade wire wool will also remove any oil soap from them.

It is well worth spending some time cleaning up the fretboard and frets after any fretting work, as it will make the whole setup feel really great, either on your own guitar or on a customer's. It comes back to the philosophy of getting in and doing the job and getting out like you have never been there!

With the frets all levelled, re-crowned and polished, the guitar needs to be given a new set of strings and brought back up to pitch. Once it is up to pitch, the neck relief needs to be assessed. If the neck was straight and did not need adjusting, the relief should go back to exactly where it was before. This should mean that the setup

The initial polishing-out gets rid of any black ink.

be reduced, along with the string height at the 12th fret, and the nut to 1st fret height will need to be trimmed.

Tips

Over the years, I have completed many fret dresses, as well as teaching fret dressing as a standalone course and as part of a longer build course, so I have inevitably picked up lots of tips from observing students' struggles as well as reviewing my own mishaps. When doing the job for the first time, it is important to make sure that you have the theory down in practice on the frets. Visually, it will be obvious whether you understand the processes and are able to work with the tools to achieve the desired goal.

When crowning, aim for a good clean solid line at the top of the fret. Do not worry about how fine that line is at the start. If you look for completion at the very beginning on the first fret, you will probably spend 10 or 15 minutes trying to get it better and better, and once you have done it, you still have 21 frets to go! Bringing them all in slowly, experiencing a sense of repetition with the file, and finding the right angles will instill in your muscle memory a deeper understanding of how to get the file to work for you. By the time you reach the last fret you will have developed enough confidence to go back and make those first few frets even better. Going back to the first frets and getting straight to that biting point with the file will bring the line on the top of the fret nicely in and thinner and thinner.

Beginners often put too much pressure on the diamond fret file. When I was starting out, my index finger used to hurt so much that I had to put masking tape

Polished-out frets look great and will be great to play on.

is still good. However, the amount of fret taken off does come into the re-setup. If there has been only a small amount of levelling to do, the setup is usually fine. Where some major indents have been corrected, the neck relief might need bringing in and the bridge height may need adjusting. It is rare that the nut will need some filing to get it down to a good nut to 1st fret height, but if a lot of fret height has been taken down, this may be necessary. In those cases, though, it would be quite common for the neck relief to have been quite high to help the setup, with the aim of getting around those indented frets and any overtones or buzzing. With the frets all perfect and the strings back to pitch, if the same amount of relief is put into the neck as before the fret dress, the neck will inevitably have more relief than it should. The relief will need to around it. It was a bit like the pain you get when you are learning to play those first few chords. Too much pressure not only hurts the fingers, but also stops the notes being in tune! Experience teaches you to allow the file to do more of the work. Filing uses different muscles from many normal activities, and the repetitive movements can make the wrist or forearm quite uncomfortable. In this case, if you find yourself struggling and tensing up, it is important to take a break from it. Many guitarists find it difficult initially. Knowing that dressing the frets will make the guitar play and sound the best it has for quite some time can be your motivation.

Be wary of being in a rush and just trying to get the job done as quickly as possible. I have certainly learnt from experience that frustration can easily creep in when you are on a deadline. If you have removed the neck from the body and placed it on the bench, and are filing back and forth, bass to treble, at speed, it is quite likely that you will fall off the fretboard when filing back towards your body on the bass side and then hit the bench with the file. Before you can stop yourself, you will be heading back towards the bass side of the neck with the file in your hand and will knock into the neck.

Students so often do this when they are rushing their work, even though they have been warned against it. In a room full of people fret dressing it is really noticeable and audible: the file hitting the pad on the bench and then a millisecond later a little knock on the guitar's neck. The ding in the neck is always perfectly under the tang of the fret. These minor knocks can sometimes be polished out; satin finishes are quite receptive to this, but others are less so. The problem can be avoided by putting your thumb in the way, on the side of the neck under the fret that you are filing. If you fall off the fretboard, either through going too quickly or through a lack of concentration, the file will fall on your thumb and usually into your thumbnail, causing pain – quite an effective deterrent! Going by the book, you should not have your thumb in that position and you should not be hurting yourself when fret dressing. Going at a comfortable pace for your experience and ability is key. That said, I do still tend to have my thumb in the way, but I have not hit it for a long time!

It is also easy to fall off the higher frets on a set-neck guitar, such as a Les Paul or similar, and especially on a single-cut body. The 14th to 21st frets on the bass side have the body up against the fretboard so the angle for filing is slightly hindered, although most guitars of this style have a flatter radius board, at 12in, 14in or 16in. The difficulty is getting the bass side of the fret filed well; it can certainly be done but it is trickier. Another obstacle in your way is the three-way toggle switch on most Les Paul styles, which makes it very difficult to get a good clean angle on the 20th and 21st frets. Unscrewing the switch and letting it drop into its cavity, usually with it still poking out, helps get around this. The top of the body can be prepared with some cardboard to protect it against a file falling off the fret, but even a little knock on the cardboard can result in a visible mark on the top of the guitar, especially if it is finished with nitrocellulose lacquer. Turning the guitar around and coming at the bass sides of the fret from the treble will help remove some more black ink and get the crown better. The best method is just to go slowly and be super-careful in this area. You may also want to consider StewMac's curved diamond file, which claims to give better access.

Anything to do with frets falls within the realms of lutherie, which is a craft and an art, requiring specific tools and always improving with experience. The more you do, the better the job will be, for sure.

CHAPTER 18

Re-Fretting

Understanding re-fretting

Re-fretting is almost certainly the hardest job on the repair books, requiring specialist skills and experience. It is very rewarding, however, and other jobs can be incorporated at the same time, so it can be a good earner for the professional guitar tech. It can also be very time-consuming (with some hours being unbillable), as well as very frustrating. No two re-frets are the same!

A re-fret is needed when there is simply not enough height left in the frets to be able to carry out a fret dressing (levelling and re-crowning, *see* Chapter 17). This is often due to the frets having been fret dressed a few times and new indents appearing. Sometimes, customers fancy trying out a different fret wire and ask for the frets to be changed even if the existing ones are not too worn. Older and vintage instruments that are still earning their keep will need re-fretting at some stage. The procedure can de-value a vintage instrument for a period of time, but it

Some of the fretting tools.

does mean that the guitar can be worked hard for many more years.

During a re-fret, all the frets are removed, the fretboard is planed or sanded and then the new frets are installed and dressed, and the guitar is set up again. Often, along with the re-fret, other repairs or modifications may be required – perhaps a new nut or a shim under the nut – and this can be done at the same time. Sometimes, the lacquer on a maple-lacquered neck may need to be refinished. This is a relatively expensive repair, as well as being one of the more difficult jobs to do, especially when the finish around the neck is checked or cracked too. Regardless of the cost, however, a re-fret will generally require some or all of these additional repairs. Any re-fret would also include getting the guitar fully set up afterwards.

A proper re-fretting job will require all the frets to be removed. Fretwork should not be done partially – it does not make sense and will not save time or money in the long run. Customers often ask for just a few of their worn frets to be replaced with new fret wire, but it is not good practice. For a start, even if they match in terms of the width and the original crown height, the new frets will inevitably have to be taken down quite significantly to be level with the old. Even if old frets higher up the neck do not look indented, they will be lower than the original crown height and any new frets will feel a lot higher, so will have to be levelled to match. This means taking a lot of life out of the new frets and, after a few months of play, indents will no doubt reappear.

Without removing all the frets, it is not possible to plane and sand the fretboard. Wear in the open-chord area on the fretboard will be particularly noticeable on rosewood and removing the frets offers an opportunity to restore the board as much as possible. A better-planed fretboard makes for a better fret job.

A decade or so ago, a lovely customer from France, who often holidayed in the South Downs and brought his guitars to the workshop, came in with a 1950s Gibson. He felt it needed a re-fret, and it certainly did, with three different types of fret wire on the fretboard. During its lifetime, it had been partially fretted a couple of times, but the frets above the 15th fret were original. Maybe its previous owners had enjoyed some more play time without the financial outlay of a complete re-fret, but the differing heights and widths had resulted in a guitar that was awkward to play. Re-fretting it properly transformed the guitar and may even have added value to it as an old Gibson.

Heating the frets after the fretboard has been waxed.

A re-fret is quite an undertaking for the repairer as well as for the customer, especially if it is a guitar that has been with them for years. However, once the job and any other related jobs have been done, the guitar can feel like new again – or even better, as it is still seasoned and familiar to its owner.

Tools

Tooling costs increase dramatically with any fretwork and re-fretting is by far the costliest job in terms of tools. StewMac tools, commonly used in the USA, are regarded as some of the best available. Since my days as a student, many other tools have been developed for this job in particular; some are not necessary, but some will be a great help and save time.

Fretting requires a long list of tools: fret pullers, a soldering iron to heat the frets and any glue, tang cutters, fret saws, re-fret saws, slot cleaning tool, fretting hammer, a fret bender, diamond files, fret end files, sanding block, possibly a fret press, use of an old drill press, neck support, notched straight edge and a straight edge. All your other tools may well be needed too!

On average, it would probably take three or four billed re-fret jobs to recoup all the tooling costs, so it is worthwhile buying good-quality tools that will not need replacing.

Preparation

Preparation for this job is key to success. There are many processes that need to be completed prior to pulling the frets out, and then again before installing new frets. The prep is slightly different depending on the type of fretboard: finished or unfinished, bound or unbound, and the type of wood used.

With unfinished fretboards, which may be made of rosewood or ebony and either bound or not, waxing is the first preparation job. With some regular furniture wax or beeswax on your finger, rub the board either side of the fret and then repeat for all the frets up the board. When heated, this wax will help lubricate the fretboard and allow the fret to be removed cleanly and more easily than if the board has not been waxed. Advice from the Gibson Repair & Restoration Shop in Nashville, USA, where my first Les Paul Custom was re-fretted, is that waxing is the best way to prep a board. Before re-fretting an ebony board, they will always wax it up as soon as it arrives and then leave it a week before doing any more work on it. Ebony can be very brittle and chip out when the frets are removed. Waxing up the board as well as heating the frets with a soldering iron, to help the wax glide into the fret slot, helps

The heated wax lubricates the fret slot for easy fret removal.

Re-applying heat to make it possible to ease the fret gently out of the slot.

a great deal in getting the frets out cleanly. Waxing works just as well on rosewood, although that wood does not tend to tear out as much as ebony.

Finished (lacquered) fretboards require much more detailed visual checking, to see whether the lacquer has lifted anywhere and how much lacquer is up the sides of the frets. Pulling the frets on a finished maple board can crack and split the lacquer, so it is a good idea to have a conversation with the customer about how the lacquer may need to be refinished. There are ways to reduce the risk of this happening and, as long as it has

been thoroughly prepped, it may be fine. If the lacquer is carefully scored with a very sharp blade right at the bottom of each side of every fret, pulling the frets should not cause any of it to lift. If there is no checking and the lacquer appears to be in good condition, it is worth giving the board a good clean with a pump polish to remove any dirt. This should be done before lifting the frets, so as not to disrupt any of the lacquer.

If it is possible to remove the neck, this will make both the handling and any refinishing a lot easier. Almost all finished maple necks and fretboards will be bolt-on style.

Removing the frets

Once the fretboard has been prepped, the frets can be removed. Using a soldering iron that preferably has a blunt tip, carefully heat the fret, working the tip across the fret wire from bass to treble side. For added protection, you can use a fret guard over the fret and on the fretboard, in case the soldering iron falls off. A well-used and unattractive solder tip generally helps stop that happening too. The fret guard may get a little waxy and dirty, but it will protect the fretboard. After a few re-frets the action with the soldering iron improves and it it will not always be necessary to use a fret guard.

With an unfinished board such as rosewood that has been waxed beforehand you should start to see the wax heat up and bubble, falling into the slot. This will allow the fret to pull out fairly easily. Using the fret pullers, pinch at the end of the fret, bass or treble side, getting just under the end of the fret at the tang nearest the edge of the board. Once they are under the end of the

fret, gently open the fret pullers just enough to be able to move further into the fret by the distance between it and the next tang – around 0.050in (1mm) – and then pinch again. Move gently along in these small increments to lift the fret gradually with each pinch. Moving the pullers too far each time across the fret tends to lead to more tear-out (tiny chips in the wood). Once the pullers are all the way over the other side of the fret, the final bit of fret should just pull up and out of the fret slot very easily. Ideally, the amount of tear-out will be very minimal when the fretboard has been prepped and the frets have been pulled in this way. When working on an unfinished board, keep any tear-out, as this can be used to make some dust for filling any part of the board nearest to where the tang has come out.

If you are pulling the frets on a finished board, heating them up will help move any glue that has been used. Again, use the fret guard for protection. If the finish is to be removed once all the frets are out, there is less focus on the lacquer chipping. If the lacquer has checked or cracked, especially if it is the heavy poly type, remove some of it first. On one example of a 1970s Stratocaster in the workshop, the lacquer was quite well lifted and cracked all over the fretboard. Before pulling the frets, and using a very thin feeler gauge, it was possible to get under the cracked lacquer and chip it off easily. Once all the frets were out, the fretboard was very close to being ready to be lightly sanded to even out the lacquer over the entire board as well as clean up the maple. This needed doing especially at the open-chord positions, where the lacquer had gone through some years before and was quite dirty. It was not possible to remove all that dirt, but the result was a nice sympathetic restoration rather than a brand-new-looking fretboard on a vintage neck.

Frets removed cleanly from a 1970s Stratocaster.

Gibson nibs

Gibson fretboards are most commonly bound and have been produced for years with plastic ends to the frets called 'nibs'. Retaining the nibs during a re-fret is very difficult and ultimately much more time-consuming than a standard re-fret, so the job will need to be priced accordingly.

With the frets fitted to the fretboard prior to the binding being fitted, it is then glued up with the plastic binding at the same height as the fret, proud of the fretboard and then the plastic in between the frets is filed down, often scraped in the early days, which is why you can sometimes see file marks on the bindings. It is a quicker way of producing a bound fretboard than when a bound board is initially fretted from scratch, or when a bound fretboard needs re-fretting.

Whether you like the binding nibs or not, they are an element of re-fretting that needs to be discussed with the owner. Most customers are happy to have them removed rather than paying double or triple the standard charge for a re-fret. The added cost is due to the time it takes to cut each fret to the exact measurement of the distance between the plastic binding nibs, and to get the fret well seated without cracking the nibs. Time is also needed to ensure that there are no gaps between the nibs and the new frets. If necessary, filler can be used to bridge any

Gibson binding nibs.

gaps. Heating the nibs a little can help, but, as the fretboard cannot be planed or sanded, it will be impossible to do a really good re-fret job. The likelihood of breaking a few nibs makes it very tough, too. With the nibs sanded down and the fretboard nice and cleaned up, the re-fret becomes a great deal easier. There is an added benefit, too, in that the width of the playing area on the fret is increased.

There have been many occasions when customers have complained about the High E string falling off the fret and into a gap between the fret and the nib. This tiny gap is just right to accommodate a High E string, which can be very frustrating. Some filing of the fret end into the nib does help, but if the nibs are removed during a re-fret, it will no longer be an issue.

Removing the nibs can devalue some Gibsons, but retaining them, removing the plastic binding and re-fitting the board in the way it was produced originally will be extremely time-consuming and costly, and may even devalue the instrument too.

Pulling the frets on a bound board is essentially the same process. The frets will usually overhang the binding and the fret pullers need to get under the fret end to pinch and pull them.

With the frets removed, the fretboard needs cleaning up. If there has been any tear-out (tiny chips in the wood), this needs filling with some corresponding wood and superglue before sanding and planing. It will usually occur with rosewood or ebony and a small offcut from a wood supplier should make enough fine

dust, sanded off with a block with some 320-grit sandpaper or a spindle sander and collected on a clean flat surface, such as a radius gauge. The dust is mixed with superglue to make a paste, which is then applied with a micro-chisel to fill any tear-out.

Adding a fine veneer in the fret slot can help stop any of the filler paste getting too deep. A glue accelerator will help speed up the curing time. It is worth checking with the new fret wire whether the width of the fret will cover any noticeable marks

in the wood where the tang has been pulled out. The fret wire usually covers most marks.

An unfinished board can be planed with 320-grit sandpaper stuck to a levelling bar or a radius block mirroring the radius of the fretboard, to take out any imperfections. The same method can be used to chase out any minor wear in the open-chord positions. This would also be the time to reduce the binding nibs (*see* above), if appropriate. A finished board that is free of chips or cracks in the lacquer

Cleaning up the fret slots, ready for re-fretting.

Fret wire prepared for use in a few fret jobs.

could be cleaned up, too, but this is best done beforehand.

After the fretboard has been cleaned up, the fret slots need cleaning out. Sometimes, the slots will need more than just removal of dust, and a fret saw will be required to remove any glue residue. Where the board has been planed a lot, due to some significant wear, some slots may need to be deepened to accommodate the new tang depth. This is not always apparent straight away and, with some frets in and some not seating quite so well, the fret saw is needed to cut into the board, allowing the frets to sit better. A feeler gauge on an unbound fretboard can be used and marked up with a fine pencil to measure the depth of the slot. This is then checked against the tang depth. With frets being replaced like for like, this is not usually a problem. It can be more of an issue with much older guitars that have seen some wear on the fretboard or have been re-fretted before.

Fret wire

Before removing the fret wire it is best to check the width and original crown height and even the tang if possible. The nickel content ideally needs to be up to 18 per cent, neither too soft nor too hard. Stainless-steel fret wire is very hard and makes for a more difficult re-fret. More often than not, customers want to replace worn frets with fret wire that matches the original, so it might be necessary to refer to one of the online fret wire charts as well as manufacturers' spec sheets. With either a finished or unfinished fretboard, using a very slightly wider fret can help conceal where the original frets have been. The new wire does not have to be much wider – a 0.100in wire instead of 0.090in, say, will just sit over any line marked in either the finish or on the fretboard. This will be more effective on a finished board.

Crown height should also be discussed with the owner, as the old frets will be quite low, while brand-new wire will be relatively tall and can feel quite different. Some customers actually prefer a slightly lower crown height, as they put less weight and bend into the string off it. Adding a wire with a high crown height could also have an impact on the nut to 1st fret; if the job is on a budget, it is worth double-checking these numbers too. It is not always possible to get away with the original nut when re-fretting.

Once the type and width of fret wire has been chosen, the frets come delivered in two ways: straight lengths, usually bought by the weight from StewMac, or Dunlop fret wire that comes as around 25 cut lengths that are sometimes slightly radiused. The radius on the fret wire might not match the radius required to fit, so with both types a fret bender needs to be used on it. It should be over-radiused to the fretboard: a 12in fretboard needs the frets radiused at a minimum of 9.5in. If the fret is over-radiused, there will be some light in the middle under the fret when it is placed on the board. The fret will compress in the fret slot and the tang will bind inside too. When the fret is not sufficiently radiused, it may not seat very well when it is hammered in, as there may be a lack of resistance with the tang. Generally, if there are a few frets that are failing to seat as well as others, it is advisable to remove them carefully, either re-radius or over-radius them, and try again. Such issues could also be down to some slight differences in the depth or radius of the fretboard, especially if it has not been planed much before.

With a bound fretboard, the tang needs to be removed with fret tang cutters, allowing the fret to sit inside the binding. The underside of the fret should also be cleaned up using a file. The better the underside of the fret, the better the finished job. If this is not done properly, once the frets are installed and bevelled, it will be noticeable where the tang was, usually indicated by a little notch under the fret. The tang needs to be cut about 0.025in in from the binding inner edge on both sides of the fret. To measure this, place the fret in the slot bass side and see how much tang needs removing. Check the prepared fret alongside the slot and make sure it has enough space to flatten out when hammered in, without bumping into the bindings. If this happens, the tang can damage the plastic bindings, either immediately

Hammering in the first two frets, starting bass side then treble, and then slowly going across the top.

or over time with expansion, causing a fine crack, perfectly in the middle of that fret. In the worst cases, if the tang is not cut short enough or double-checked, it will simply break the binding. If the tang is cut too much inside of the slot, then it can be more difficult to get the fret seated.

This is an area that needs close attention; hopefully, your skills will improve with every fret job you do. Obviously, with unbound fretboards, it is not an issue.

Bevelling the edge of the frets.

Installing and finishing the frets

There are numerous ways to get the frets in, but I always come back to the traditional method: hammering with a good fretting hammer. A drill press with a radiused brass fret presser, pressing the frets in, and using various fret jaws all work but, after getting all the prep done – removal, preparation of the board and correct shaping of the fret wire – a fretting hammer works best. Every re-fret presents new issues and there will always be something to learn from each job. A good example of this is one customer's electric mandolin that needed a re-fretting. It was an F-style instrument, with a bound fretboard, the end of which was hanging over the caved top, and higher-register frets that were only about an inch wide. It certainly posed a challenge. Research into whether my approach should be different for a mandolin came up with some very useful advice. It was specific to fretting mandolins, but it made sense to my fret hammering generally, and I have stuck to and taught the technique ever since. The technique involves using the same gentle hammer blows, but many, many more of them. Previously, I was using maybe 10 to 20 blows to get a fret seated well, whereas this advice was suggesting 40 to 50. Approaching the customer's mandolin with this information really helped.

Another part to getting the frets hammered in well is protecting the neck and removing the movement in it. A good neck support with a nice radius inside of it really helps on all necks. Leaving the neck just in the cradle of a neck support will not reduce the bounce and can make the hammering less efficient.

When using superglue (Satellite City Green), the fretboard should be protected with a bit of wax. When using wood glue (Titebond), any seepage can be cleaned up either during or after the application. Put a small amount in the slot. Bring the cut and radiused fret over the slot and, holding it firmly, begin to tap it gently in, first on the bass side of the fret and then on the treble side. Once the two sides are well seated – not fully, but enough to hold the fret securely – you can start to hammer gently using the brass end of a fretting hammer, softer than the fret itself. Working from bass to treble in small increments, the fret will begin to seat further. There will be a subtle but noticeable change in the sound when the fret is well seated in the fret slot. As it hits the board nice and evenly, it will give off a deeper tone.

All the frets need seating the same. It does get easier and takes a little less time towards the top part of the fretboard, with either a bolt-on neck that can be removed from the body and placed on the bench, or with a fixed neck. The tongue part of the fretboard, usually 14th fret and up, is very rigid and there is minimal bounce when hammering in the frets. Once the frets are installed, a good visual check of how well they have seated is worthwhile. If there is one that is not quite right, it is better to sort it out now rather than finding out when you come to fret dressing and levelling. Sometimes, a little more hammering will be enough. Removing the fret and cleaning out the slot again can also help, as can re-radiusing the fret. Always be careful of removing a newly installed fret on woods such as ebony or rosewood, as there may still be some tear-out.

If superglue has been used, an accelerator can ensure that it is nicely set; wood glue takes a little longer. A blunt chisel or a razor will help remove any excess. Once the frets are in, any seepage should be cleaned up before it gets too set.

The fret-end overhangs now need clipping back with the fret nippers. They can be cut from the side or the top. With an unbound fretboard, working from side to side works well and crimps the fret nicely. On a bound fretboard, cutting the overhang from the top down at the body join is sometimes the only way to get the ends

off. Either way, the ends then need to be filed flush to the fretboard edge or binding edge, before introducing a bevel edge to them. The better this is done, with no fret overhanging, the quicker and better the bevel will come. The binding and edge of the fretboard cannot be touched, but the fret ends need to be at a very good 90 degrees. Some masking tape up the side of the fretboard and/or binding can help but most tools are fairly kind and get the fret ends really nice and close.

Running up and down the bass and treble side with a good bevelled-edge file at 35 degrees will create an edge that looks good and feels decent too. Once this has been done, any metal burrs will need to be filed away, to remove any sharp edges. A little round over-file is the best tool for this – you can get in quite a nice rhythm just gently smoothing over the ends.

This is an area where luthiers tend to have differing views on style. I like fret ends to be finished quite traditionally, but others like to give them a more rounded finish, perhaps to make them feel very smooth and unobtrusive, or perhaps because they simply prefer the aesthetic. Of course, more important than the personal taste of the luthier is the satisfaction of the customer. With some effort, the round over file can do a good job, but the process of fret dressing, re-crowning and then polishing out will also help round over any sharpness.

With any re-fret, the new frets will need dressing afterwards. This is usually much easier than dressing used and worn-out frets. With the preparation of the neck and the frets seated well and evenly, the job of levelling the frets should be very quick. There may be some frets that are less well seated, and this will be highlighted by more height coming off them than off others. However, it is not usually

very much and is obviously a necessity to ensure that all the frets are level with one another. Re-crowning new frets is also easier. With only a small amount of levelling being required, and therefore the tops of the frets not being too wide, crowning takes less time and effort. This is an opportunity to make sure the ends of the frets crown well to the bevelled edge, and to remove any remaining sharp edges.

After the crowning, the frets need to be polished up, as with a fret dress, but with some extra consideration to the ends. The round over file can be useful here again. Once the guitar is strung and up to pitch, and the neck relief is back to specs, it is left in the rack overnight, allowing everything to settle before checking again. If the nut to 1st fret is too low, due to the additional crown height of the new frets, this can be resolved by shimming the nut, putting a veneer under it, or getting into replacing it. Hopefully, the decision will have been made before starting the fretwork. Sometimes placing a shim under the nut, using a 0.3mm or 0.5mm maple veneer, can be a fix for the reduced nut to 1st fret height or will give a good indication of how much extra height is required for a new nut. (For advice on replacing a nut, *see* Chapter 14.)

With the setup checked and in a good place, the frets are reviewed by consistently fretting each one, up and down the fretboard, playing each note with the same level of attack. Each fret should be playing cleanly with no overtones and the ends of the frets should be feeling nice, with no sharpness over the entire board. For an unfinished board, a final clean with 0000-grade wire wool and fretboard soap or conditioner, prior to stringing up, will finish the job. A good pump polish will get a maple board cleaned up well. For a fretboard that needs lacquering prior to re-fretting, *see* Chapter 20.

CHAPTER 19

Broken Headstocks

Gibson ES335 headstock break (front).

Gibson ES335 headstock break (back).

Breaks and break angles

Sadly, as an authorised Gibson Service Centre, 12th Fret repair shop sees many Gibson neck breaks in for repair – and they are not covered by warranty, by the way! Any headstock that has a break angle behind the nut can break if the guitar is dropped, whether it is in the case or not. The mahogany necks on Gibsons are in most cases made from one piece of wood with a 14- or 17-degree headstock break angle. The break angle exists for a few reasons: if it is over the nut, the strings have a good leading edge out of the nut, and it also gives a particular aspect to the tone of the guitar. Epiphones and other similar instruments have a similar headstock break angle, tending to have a scarf joint at the headstock and possibly the heel of the neck too. This is because they can use two or three smaller pieces of wood to make the neck, which is more cost-effective. It is very rare that the break is at the scarf joint, however; most will break in the same way as a Gibson. While it may be heart-breaking for an owner, as a repairer, a headstock break is very much a bread-and-butter job – a workshop may see as many as three or four a month.

There has been some debate over the years as to why Gibson do not fix this issue. Basically, it stems from a tradition of guitar building and, even though a workshop may repair dozens over the course

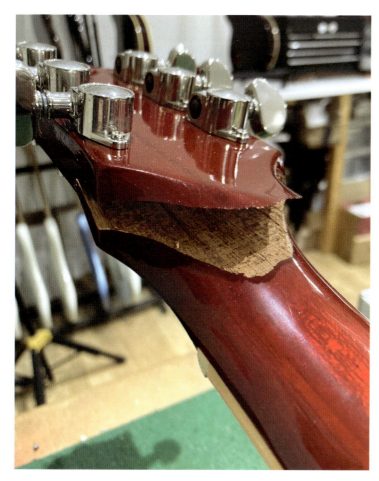

A headstock break on an ES335 is a fairly common occurrence.

done right. The gold finish was a bit much for a spray can. It was left to a finishing company who did a great job mixing and matching the paint. The end result was a fully concealed repair, with the Dave Grohl signature saved. Luckily, the insurance company paid out on that occasion – it was a very high repair bill!

The headstock on my very first Gibson Les Paul Standard broke while I was at a band practice and this is one of the reasons why, some years later, I decided to go to the USA to study lutherie. This lovely black 1990 Les Paul had fallen off my back in between songs. I had thought it was well locked in on the strap's buttons, but sadly the top strap button let go of the strap, and it landed on the floor and broke. I was very upset. It was 'fixed' at my local shop, but a few months later the crack reappeared and it had to go back to be repaired again. A few weeks later, the same happened again. There were very few guitar shops or luthiers around at the time, so I had no choice about where to take it. The shop decided to chisel out some wood, put two Allen keys in the back of the headstock, cover that with a load of filler and then apply a bit of black paint to conceal what they had done. Although it looked okay to start with, within a few weeks, these two very hard objects began to appear. I dug them out and the guitar went into its case for some years. At least ten years later, a very good friend suggested I should learn how to fix that guitar properly, and maybe even learn how to build guitars. My negative experience with that headstock is part of the motivation behind my subsequent career, and this book!

Unlike Gibsons, broken headstocks on Fenders are very rare. I have only ever seen one: a Telecaster, owned by a famous punk rock band from New York who were touring in the UK. The guitar

of a few years, Gibson are producing at least 500 guitars a day, which means that relatively few are suffering breaks. There is also a view that a guitar can actually be improved by this type of break. When the weakest point on the guitar is broken and repaired well, it no longer has that weak point and should not be at risk of the headstock breaking in the same place again. One example of a positive attitude to this was a very good customer whose dog knocked his Les Paul Standard off its stand. Realising that the headstock had broken, the owner was genuinely looking forward to how the repair might change the tone of the guitar. Unlike many customers, he did not need counselling or support to get over the break. The guitar repaired very well, and he was delighted.

Another example – not the easiest job by any stretch of the imagination – was a touring guitar that belonged to an artist in a large Foo Fighters tribute band. Headlining a festival in Spain, he had a Pelham Blue DG335 and a Gold Dave Grohl DG335 in a double stand next to him. The stand got caught on a lead or similar and started to fall and he had to decide very quickly which one to save. He chose the Pelham Blue; the Gold hit the stage, and pop went the headstock. Normally, it would have been a regular repair job but this one not only had a deep Gold flake finish, but was also signed by Dave Grohl himself on the back of the headstock, right where it had broken. The value of the guitar was significantly affected by the break, but retaining the signature was key to getting the job was apparently thrown quite high in the air and when it landed the headstock area cracked. It was brought to the workshop by their guitar tech in between a few gigs. There was a fine hairline crack that ran from the nut to the top of the headstock. There were some other, very minor signs of damage that had been caused when it fell, but they were not really an issue with this touring guitar. With the machine heads off and the crack prised open a little with a couple of feeler gauges, the Titebond glue went easily into the crack, and a small clamp was fitted. After a few hours waiting for the glue to bond, the guitar went back on tour! It was certainly an easier and quicker repair process than the typical Gibson-style headstock break.

With this type of repair, it is definitely worth having a conversation with the customer about whether the repaired headstock break needs refinishing or not. The refinishing usually doubles the cost of the repair and there is no guarantee that the break will be fully concealed. With most 'clean' breaks, the re-glued neck will look absolutely fine without any major refinishing. If proper care and attention are given to how much pressure is needed (doing some dry runs will help), and some very fine wet-sanding is done to make sure the repair feels smooth to touch and unnoticeable during play, it is unlikely that any lacquer will be needed. Many headstock repairs do not need any finishing, but it must be discussed with the customer beforehand, either via email with photos or in person. In recent years, it seems that more customers have been asking asked for a break repair to be refinished and concealed, perhaps with darker colours or, where there is a dark burst around the neck to body join, adding a burst into the neck and headstock area. Darkening cherry reds in the area can help mask a repair. On some repairs, the whole of the back of the headstock has been sprayed black to a point that finishes just below the break – similar to how some of the old Gibson Archtops were made – and this can look very good. Spraying some clear nitrocellulose lacquer over the repair can conceal it. Certainly, it will be less discernible to touch and can also look very good in some lights, although a hairline crack will usually be visible beneath the lacquer. The majority of breaks will have a negative effect on the value of a guitar. The idea of trying to conceal the repair is less about trying to hide the fact that there has been a broken headstock, and more about trying to make the repair look good.

Preparation, repair, polishing and buffing

As soon as a guitar comes in with a broken headstock, the first thing to do is to get the strings off, as well as all the machine heads, including the bushings and truss-rod cover, if it is not already off or broken. This stops any hardware getting in the way when the time comes to use clamps. Once it is clear of washers, screws or bushings, the headstock face and the back of the area can be protected using multiple layers of card or cork blocks.

With most Gibsons, the rest of the hardware should be transferred to a box, along with the machine heads. With nearly all headstock repairs, it is worth giving all the hardware a polish, especially if the break is going to be treated to some refinishing, which tends to make the guitar look very new. Cleaning up the hardware with some 0000-grade wire wool will bring it all to a good shine, so that it matches better with the brand-new appearance of the back of the head and neck. More commonly, the headstock will be just opened up, with minimal creasing to the front-head veneer or facing, and the truss-rod cover will sometimes be bent or cracked. Sometimes, the headstock will be attached just by the strings and removing the strings will detach it from the rest of the guitar, although this is less common.

The headstock area front and back can be prepared to accept a couple of F clamps with pieces of hard cardboard and some thin offcuts of maple, and the damage repaired using Titebond Original wood glue. As the headstock area on all Gibsons is angled, it can take some time to get the pressure in the right places. With the guitar upside down on the bench, or sometimes over the end of the bench, to get a good view from all angles, it helps to do a few dry runs to mask up the protective pieces and mark the clamp positions. The aim is to

Some light pressure is applied to open up the break, ready for the glue to be applied.

identify when the position and clamping pressure are such that the headstock meets the lower part of the neck, and feels really flush. The better it feels at this stage, the less making good will be required afterwards.

Having confirmed the best position for the clamps and ensured that the closing of the break all over the area feels as good as it can be, the glue can be applied. This can be done using a pipette or syringe, but it is also possible to get the glue deep inside the break by holding the guitar up, resting on the shoulder, and pressing it lightly against the side of the bench (ideally with some form of protection so as not to scratch the top of the headstock). With

a little forward movement, the break in the headstock will open up fairly easily, allowing glue to be squeezed in slowly. The effect of gravity will take it deep inside the break. This method is particularly useful for someone who is working on their own, and can be helped further by the use of some fine feeler gauges or a pipette, to push the glue in until you get the desired result.

Any seepage of wood glue is easily cleaned up, even if it comes through the truss-rod cavity and on to the face. It is best not to get too much glue in contact with the material that is being used to protect the headstock face, in case it bonds with that too. It should come off cleanly,

but it would be better to avoid it in the first place.

With the glue fully in, pressure needs to be applied, initially by hand and then using the clamps to hold the area before adding some more pressure. The pressure with the F clamps can be quite significant, so it is important to double-check the area and make sure that they are well positioned on the protection. If this is not done carefully, marks may show up either on the back of the head or the face. To gauge the amount of glue that is needed, have a look at the seepage. If you have to scoop out the excess, that is a good sign. Use your fingers to get around and underneath the clamps, removing enough glue

Pressure with the hand is enough to squeeze out some of the excess glue.

The F clamps are rested on some heavy-duty card and pressure is applied.

so that you can feel the area and make sure that it is clamped with enough pressure, and that it feels smooth, with no ridge in the break.

With the area cleaned up as well as it can be, the guitar can be left on the bench or carefully placed in the rack and ideally allowed to settle overnight. The glue tends to bond within a few hours, but leaving the guitars overnight or over the weekend gives the repair a chance to work properly. Headstock repair was always a job to be done at the end of the week, and then the guitars were clamped up and left over the weekend, away from any curious eyes or hands. It did mean buying loads of clamps, though!

Once the glue is fully bonded, the clamps and protective materials can be removed, and the area can be cleaned up using a small amount of water and some blue workshop towel. The front of the headstock and all around the neck underneath the nut needs to be completely clean of any glue before doing some fine sanding to smooth over the area, if required. Having undertaken a few dry runs to ensure that the clamping pressure is just right, hopefully the break area will already feel smooth once the glue has been cleaned up. Sometimes, there will be a small, slightly rough area on one side or the other, or it may just feel noticeable across the join, like a little bump. This can be improved by using some fine wet and dry sandpaper, of 500- or 1000-grit, with a little buffing or polishing to bring back to a shine. With a little water with a tiny drop of washing up liquid in it, in an old pump polish pot, spray the back of the neck and gently sand the area in a circular motion until it feels nice and smooth.

Starting with 500-grit paper, work that and then follow with 1000-grit paper, then 1500-, 2000- and 3000-grit, if you have them. This will leave the back of the headstock feeling very good to touch. It can then be polished up, either with a cream polish or with a very light buffing on the buffing wheel with some fine-grade polish. This can be done if the repair is very clean. If it needs a little touching in, as most repairs will, some clear lacquer can be used just to 'drop fill' the hairline crack – the area between the repair, which is a very small sunken area as opposed to a ridge. Delivered either via a pipette or sprayed on to the end of a fine screwdriver, lacquer can be gently placed on the hairline crack and, once hardened, lightly sanded as before.

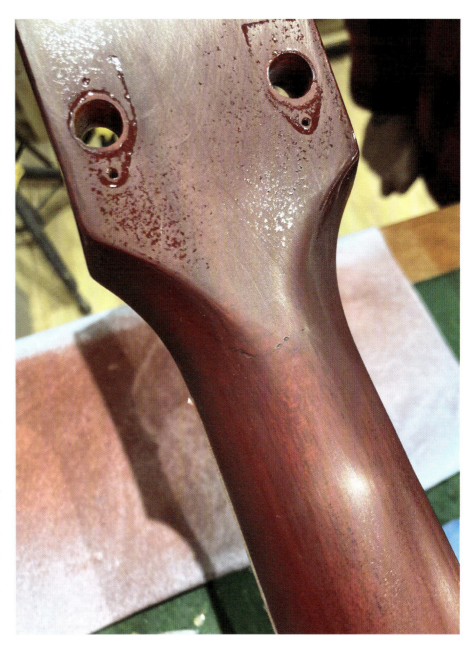

Once the headstock area has been cleaned up, there may be a couple of indents that need filling with lacquer.

If the repair needs only the smallest amount of lacquer, a little overspray can be applied, just to improve the feel rather than fully refinishing it. The area can then be wet-sanded up to 1000-grit or higher, and a few coats of clear sprayed over it may be all that is needed for the lacquer to sit properly over the top. Once it is fully hardened and wet-sanded, the area can be polished, or buffed and polished, to finish the job.

When the aim is to carry out the repair and fully conceal the break as much as possible, the process of gluing and clamping is exactly the same, but the time spent preparing the area is even more important. If the back of the headstock feels very smooth before it is coloured and has clear coats applied, the end result will be better. Some hairline cracks are deeper than they appear and sometimes the lacquer just does not want to sit well, but such issues can be prevented if a good surface is created.

Usually, the area needs a little bursting in with a darker colour. A repair on a translucent cherry red guitar is notoriously difficult to conceal, but a very light burst of either a darker red or cherry and then several coats of the original cherry can make it slowly fade from sight. Once the colour is fully hardened, it is best to very lightly wet-sand the area with 3000-grit – the higher the grit, the less likely it is to remove the colour, although some removal can help to blend the colour. It is all too easy to take the colour back a little too much and then to have to reapply, so caution is advised here. Make sure you are happy with the colour and the bursting of the area before applying the clear top coats. Some vintage sunburst finished guitars, particularly ES335s and the like, tend to have a very dark burst into the heel of the neck as it joins the body. A headstock repair can be an opportunity to do a very similar dark burst around the back of the neck into the headstock area where the hairline crack is visible. A few light mist sprays over the repaired area with some black lacquer or some vintage dark brown can look very good and conceal the break. Once this has dried and has been very lightly sanded back, the clear coats can be layered up to build a good amount of lacquer. This is allowed to cure and, with wet-sanding from 1000-grit to 2000 grit and then finally 3000-grit, the repair should be fully concealed. The finish could be buffed by hand at this stage, perhaps with some light cutting compound and

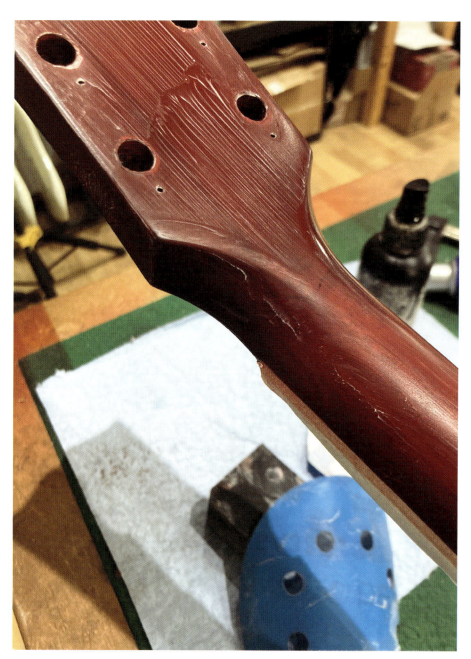

Wet-sanding.

blue workshop towel or a good cloth. If you have access to a buffing arbour, you can buff with a fine cutting compound and then finish with a high-gloss compound on the buffing wheel. This would also be the time to buff the rest of the back of the headstock area and down the neck. In almost all breaks, the front face of the headstock may show some very light creases, which can also be buffed. Buffing out the entire neck will give it a great appearance and make the repaired area seem less noticeable. When going to such lengths with this sort of repair, it is worth giving the body a good buff and buff polish too, then the whole guitar will look like new.

More severe breaks

Dealing with more severe breaks, especially when the headstock has come clean off, requires a little more prep and effort, to get a feeling for how best the two pieces should go back together. In some cases, the wood fibres will need some adjustment, maybe some removing. A micro-chisel can be used to score the area a little, making a better contact point. A light tap (or several taps) with the plastic end of a fretting hammer can get the headstock fitting better, closing up the gap, which is usually most visible on the headstock face. With a more demanding repair, the gap around the front, often around the two outer E string machine-head holes, will need some filler. Two-pack car filler generally seems to work better than a standard wood filler, although Osmo Wood Filler works especially well on small areas. The two-pack car filler is made up of a filler and a hardener and can really fill the gap on the headstock face if there are large chunks of wood or heavy lacquer missing. This product is probably best on poly finishes, as the chips and break require a lot more filling.

Once the filler has fully hardened, which does not take too long, it can be sanded with an orbit sander to flatten it.

With some masking tape over the logo on the guitar or any other piece of pearl or celluloid, the area can be sprayed (usually black) and then clear coats can be applied over the top. This usually produces a great end result, where the join between the two pieces is not noticeable. It should look like it did originally.

The back of the neck does not usually need much filling, so wood filler will be better than two-part car filler. Home DIY wood filler that is designed for use on, say, skirting boards does not work very well. A product that has been designed for use on guitars is best and Osmo is a highly recommended brand.

On the rare occasions when the head veneer is an ebony facing, using an ebony paste will work well. This is created by sanding some ebony with fine sandpaper and mixing it with superglue to make the paste. Once set, it can be sanded down and then up through the grits, until it is very smooth. With clear coats over the top, the repair should be very well concealed.

Buffing the headstock sides after wet-sanding the clear lacquer.

Buffing the back of the neck after wet-sanding.

Even with a hairline crack remaining visible, the repair is smooth to the touch and the overall finish is nice.

There are other methods for dealing with a more severe break. One is to make some cleats and to insert them into two small channels routed out in the back of the neck and headstock area. They are then sanded back, filed and finished. The direction of the wood grain must be taken into consideration, to make the repair very strong, and you need a jig to rout out the channels. The repair will be solid, but routing or chiselling out the channels does seem risky and time-consuming. Also, the neck will still need gluing up in the same manner prior to inserting the cleats, so it is doubling up on the work a little.

Another method that I learned while spending some time at the Gibson Repair & Restoration Shop in Nashville involves the same gluing and clamping up of the neck but, once the glue has set, a small channel is mill-filed around the break area to accommodate some 1in-wide carbon-fibre ribbon. The carbon-fibre ribbon, with an epoxy soaked into it, is pulled tightly around the back of the headstock and neck area. This sets very hard and can then be shaped to the original headstock area, sanded up to a high-grit paper, and lacquered. The end result is a well-concealed repair

that is more or less invisible, especially with a burst in the area or if the guitar has a solid finish. It is also very strong. It is usually possible to put some flex in the standard repaired neck, but the carbon-repaired neck does not flex at all. I tried this repair a couple of times and it was certainly very strong, but it was much more time-consuming than the standard version and therefore more expensive for the customer. Whereas the Gibson Repair & Restoration Shop could charge well into the high hundreds, in the UK it was not economically viable.

The repair is hard to see once the area has been all buffed and polished.

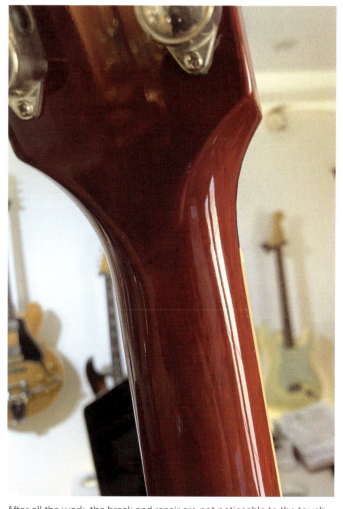

After all the work, the break and repair are not noticeable to the touch.

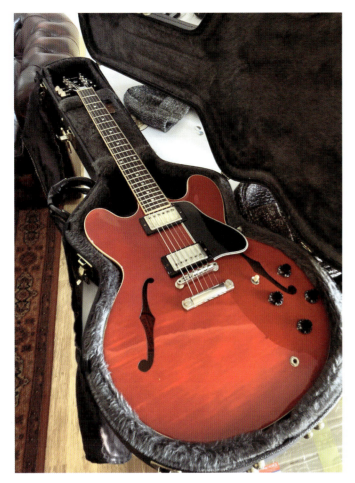

Buffing all over makes for a great finish to the job.

Wet-sanded and buffed, the headstock no longer shows any signs of damage.

Restoring the setup

Once the repair is complete, whether the break has just been glued up or whether there has been some refinishing, it is always good to do a final clean and polish on the guitar and to get it well set up. This is mainly to ensure that the truss rod is working as it should and that the guitar is nice and stable. Often, the break will have occurred when the guitar was at pitch and that may have jarred the neck relief, so getting the guitar back up to pitch and observing the relief coming back into the neck and settling is important. Usually, the guitar will be left overnight and the relief will be checked the next day. Hopefully, a little tighten on the truss rod will show that all is functioning as it should be. Sometimes, where there has been a little glue seepage in that area, adjusting the truss rod could free the nut and thread of any glue that was not cleaned up as it was being set.

Going through the rest of the setup will ensure that the guitar performs well again and feels great. The happy customer will be delighted that their guitar has been fixed and that it also looks terrific. Minor hairline cracks are to be expected, but they are much more acceptable when the rest of the guitar looks stunning.

CHAPTER 20

Finishing

Spraying

For many years in the repair shop, there were few requests for full re-sprays or even for a re-spray of the body or neck only. Just a few customers a year would ask about this type of work, and I would always refer them to a finishing company that had been highly recommended and became well known to me. The first guitar I ever built was a Telecaster that I finished with two techniques I had been taught in the USA: a two-tone burst and clear nitro-cellulose lacquer. Both jobs were highly enjoyable to do. I really enjoyed the task of applying the clear coat, the lengthy and focused wet-sanding back to get the finish well and truly flat, and then the final buff revealing a fantastic mirror finish. Back in the UK, getting a workshop set up for finishing and refinishing in the way that I had been taught, where I could offer customers the benefit of my many hours' experience (I had also lacquered a hand-built acoustic guitar by then) was just too costly for me at the time. The tooling of the repair shop had already run into the thousands and I felt that finishing was an area that could be delegated. It was a disappointment not to be able to replicate what I had learned and enjoyed so much in the USA.

There are certain repairs that require some level of finishing, and I did do this for customers, using nitrocellulose spray cans. These worked fine, as long as the surface was sufficiently well prepared. As the repair shop grew, so did the requests for refinishing, and I did carry out a few successful body refinishes. Each time the customer was happy with the end result, but the work was so much more time-consuming in the absence of a proper spray-shop set-up.

Aerosol cans are perfect for minor finish repairs and in the UK there are a few good suppliers offering a wide range of finishes and tints. With time, it should be possible to get a good match with almost all body colours. As with all repair jobs, preparation is the key to success. For example, areas around a neck break need to be sanded smooth with 320-grit sandpaper or higher before being sanded or wet-sanded up through the grits from 600, via 1000 and 2000, up to 3000, working in a circular motion. When wet-sanding, it is helpful to spray the surface with water that has a drop of washing up liquid in it. For flat surfaces, a soft block or cork block is a good tool; for the rounder parts of the neck and back of the headstock, using the sandpaper in the hand will give instant feedback.

Once the surface has been well sanded, the spraying can start. To get the best out of a spray can, it should be shaken for quite some time, to move the colour or tint around and ensure that the lacquer and thinners are evenly distributed. The can is held a few inches away from the area being sprayed and then moved smoothly across from left to right and back again. That single pass should be enough to lightly mist the area and begin to colour it, and a few more similar passes will begin to build up the coverage. The lacquer will dry quickly, but it is important not to rush to build up the colour or to layer up clear coats. If it is forced, the lacquer can easily run, particularly when bursting two colours, which can easily run into each other. If that happens, the area will usually need re-sanding. Light even coats, with time in between for the lacquer to cure, will work much better.

Top coats of lacquer over a burst or coloured area can be applied after the colour has dried, or after any necessary very fine wet-sanding has been done. The method of application for the clear coats is the same as with the colour: slowly building up the area with multiple passes. It will take about 30 minutes for the lacquer to dry, so the job of building up these coats is usually done over the course of a day. This would be applicable for headstock breaks, refinishing the headstock facing or the back of the neck, as well as for maple fretboards following a re-fret, if required, and for all

Wet-sanding the top of the guitar with 1000-grit, to get rid of any marks.

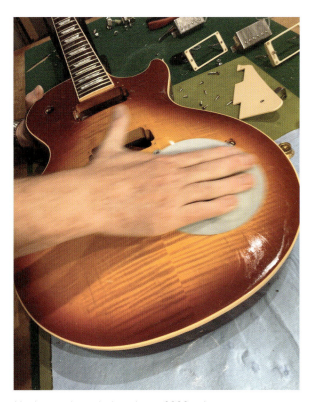

Moving up through the grits, to 2000-grit.

Wet-sanding with 3000-grit.

Wet-sanding the back with 1000- to 3000-grit can remove unsightly buckle rash.

body finish repairs. Building the lacquer up like this and then letting it cure for a few days works very well, although it can be cut back sooner. Again, learning from experience, I prefer to leave it as long as I can.

Wet-sanding

With the lacquer cured, it is time to wet-sand the area. It is sprayed with water that has a drop of washing up liquid in it, and then cut back, to get the surface as flat as it can be. Starting with 600-grit can produce the desired end result quite quickly, but there is a risk of cutting through the clear top coats. Using 1000-grit takes longer, but comes with less risk, so may be preferable. The aim with this first wet-sand is to eliminate any 'fish eyes'. This term was used a lot during my studies and refers to the shiny spots visible on the finished area – the untouched spots that the first wet-sanding has not yet reached. If they can still be seen, then more wet-sanding is required with the first sandpaper. 'Orange peel' is another term that is used to describe the slightly uneven surface exposing shiny spots around the flat spots. Working the first sandpaper well and continuing until all these spots have gone produces a much better finish later, when all the grits have been used. Sometimes, if the spots are super-fine, they can be dealt with by moving up to the next sandpaper. However, if you move on too fast, once the surface is fully wet-sanded and then buffed, they will probably still be visible, or the area will not look perfectly flat. It is really worthwhile getting the area really flat with the first grit of sandpaper.

With the first phase done properly, the rest of the wet-sanding is relatively straightforward. Moving up the grits from, say, 1000 to 1500 can be very quick, and then on to 2000-grit is the same. Once you get to 3000-grit, the area should be looking extremely good. Moving up through the grits like this will reduce the risk of going through the clear top coats of lacquer, but it is still important to be really careful on sharper edges and avoid working one spot too much. A general rule of thumb with any finishing is to sand across the whole area, both flat and uneven, and not to focus too closely on one part.

Buffing

It took me a long time to commit to getting a buffing wheel. After wet-sanding, the area of repair can be buffed by hand, with some energetic 'shoe-shining' helped by the use of a few fine cutting compounds, working up through the range. A buffer can also be used in a hand drill, although there is a risk of catching a corner of a headstock, which can lead to a sand-through, or moving the lacquer due to too much heat. As the repair shop progressed and there was more demand for finishing, a buffing arbour became a justifiable addition to the workshop. This made the next part of the process so much better.

The arbour has two buffing wheels each with different compounds to remove fine surface scratches. It has to spin at the right number of revolutions: if it is too slow, the lacquer will not buff; too quick, and the lacquer can get too hot and move around. StewMac's buffing arbour comes with a motor but there was no cost-efficient way to get powered up in the UK, so it was adapted with a simple motor from Machine Mart and a good pulley. The first compound cuts through marks from up to 2000-grit. The area is very carefully brought up to the wheel and

Buffing the top with two different compounds brings the lacquer to a great finish.

gently buffed, always moving the guitar and never allowing it to buff the same area for any length of time. With some good lighting it should be quite noticeable when the area has buffed up nicely. It should be quite shiny, with only super-fine surface scratches visible under a bright light. If that looks good, the next stage is to move up to the finer compound on the other wheel, which will remove all the fine surface scratches until the finish appears very glossy and, hopefully, mirror-like. If there are some areas that still have swirls in places, more work on the first buffing wheel is required. Much like wet-sanding, if you go to the next level before fully finishing the previous one, there will still be swirls or fish eyes visible, and the higher grit or buffing compound will not help.

Once off the buffing wheel, the area can be slightly improved even further by giving it a good clean and getting rid of any buffing wheel dust. Virtuoso Polish does not have a cutting agent and cleans the fresh lacquer very well. If the finish repair was for a headstock break, it can be blended in by lightly buffing the whole of the neck, and perhaps even the body too, if there is a discrepancy between the neck and the body because of the fresh lacquer on the neck. It will also make the guitar look great all over.

The buffing wheel works very well but there are a number of potential issues. Overheating, or 'burning', can move the lacquer around, which can set you back many hours. However, the riskiest part of buffing on a wheel is catching a corner and losing your grip on the instrument. Almost always when this happens you will catch the guitar, but for a heart-stopping moment it will seem to be heading for the floor! The headstock area is particularly tricky, with so many areas and corners to catch. Make sure the area around the buffing wheel is clear of sharp corners

Two buffing compounds that are in daily use.

Menzerna polishing compounds are very useful.

and start off lightly. As with many of the various aspects of setup and repair, the more experience you have using the tools at your disposal, the better. Spending a few hours learning how to use the buffing wheel – what works and what does not, how to handle the guitar against it, the angle at which it needs to touch the surface area, the speed at which it spins – will really help build awareness and trust. Problems usually arise through the use of a little too much force, which either causes the lacquer to move around or pushes or pulls the guitar, at worst wrenching it out of your hands. Try using an old neck and an old body for a good few hours on the wheel, to begin learning. Better they end up on the floor than a customer's or your own precious instrument!

Once it has been mastered, the buffing wheel not only reduces the time required for finishing, but also achieves a better end result than finishing by hand. Guitars that are being prepped for sale in the showroom usually all end up on the buffing wheel for about an hour, after

being very lightly wet-sanded to 3000-grit. This removes any minor defects and fine surface playing marks, so that the guitars really pop on camera and look super-fine. It is not necessary on most customer's guitars that are in the workshop for setup, but for a small additional fee they can be made to look as good as the ones hanging in the showroom.

This whole procedure – sanding the wood, layering up many coats of lacquer, waiting to cure, wet-sanding all the way up to 3000-grit and then using two different types of compound on the buffing wheel – is how all James Collins guitars are finished in house now. The process does take a few weeks, but the end result is superb. It is nice to have come full circle with these finishing skills, having enjoyed them so much while studying in the USA. My learning adventure in lutherie through the years has made me extremely grateful for the knowledge and understanding I now have, which have enabled me to reach my happy place.

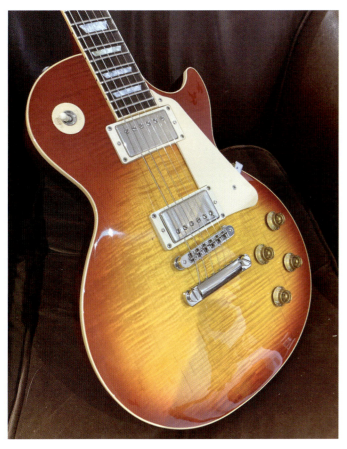

Looking like new, a 20-year-old Les Paul Standard after wet-sanding and buffing.

The back and neck after wet-sanding and buffing.

The headstock looks great too.

Close-up of the back of the Les Paul, after buffing.

James Collins Guitars Signature GTO, hand-lacquered, hand-sanded and fresh off the buffing wheel.

Index

Adjusto-Matic style bridge 33

bridge saddle radius 37–40
   adjustment 41
   checking 40–41
broken headstocks
   breaks and break angles 158–160
   more severe breaks 164–165
   polishing and buffing 162–164
   preparation and repair 160–161
   setup 166
Buzz Feiten tuning system (BFTS) 53–54

compensated tuning system 53–54

dual-action truss rod 18
Dunlop 65 59

Earvana 54
electrics
   changing pickups 134–135
   issues with
      intermittent faults and grounding
         issues 130
      lack of volume control 130–131
      output issues 130
      pickups 130
      switch issues 131
   maintenance 65–67
   replace the pots, capacitor, switches or
      jack sockets 131–134
Epiphone's bridges 32
Epiphone Tune O Matic bridge 33

Fender's Micro-Tilt system 35
Fender Stratocaster 18, 33, 46, 103–108

Fender Telecaster 41, 66
floating bridge
   balancing 45–46
   case study 46–47
   Floyd Rose bridge 47
   lift measurement 44–45
   tremolo system 43–44
Floyd Rose bridge 47
fretboard cleaning 15
   finished boards 59
   technique 59
   unfinished boards
      beeswax with turpentine 57
      0000 furniture-grade wire wool 57, 58
      lemon oil 57
      wood oil soaps 57, 58
fretboards
   cleaning
      a finished fretboard 59
      an unfinished fretboard 57–58
   maple 57
   rosewood and ebony 57
fret dressing 136–138
   levelling 141–142
   positioning 137
   preparation 139–141
   re-crowning 143–147
   tips 147–148
   tools 113, 136, 138–139
fret polishing 15, 61–63

Gibson ABR bridge 32
Gibson fretboards 153
Gibson Les Paul Standard 23–24, 96–102
   checking playability 100
   cleaning 100–101

completing setup 102
   initial assessment 96–97
   neck relief and action height
      adjustment 98–100
   setup points 97–98
   string up the guitar 101–102
Gibson-style truss rod 21
guitar repair
   broken headstocks 158–166
   buffing 169–170
   electrics
      issues with 130–131
   fret dressing 136–148
   machine heads
      issues with 126
      minor repair 126
      replacement 126–129
   nuts
      blanks 120
      finishing off 124–125
      height reduction 117–118
      issues with 115–116
      positioning of strings 120–124
      re-building 118–119
      replacing 119
   re-fretting 149–157
   repair or replace 113
   repair workbench
      drawers 110
      height 110
      instrument, photographic account
        of 111–112
      lighting 111
   spraying 167–169
   tools 112–113
   wet-sanding 169

guitar setup
    neck relief adjustment 17–27
    setup points 13–15

imperial measurements 11
intonation
    adjustment
        Fender Jazzmaster 52
        Gibson ABR 51
        in playing position 52, 53
    compensated tuning system
        53–54
    measurement 52–53
    and scale length 49–51

maintenance
    electrics 65–67
    fretboards
        cleaning 57–59
        maple 57
        rosewood and ebony 57
    fret polishing 15
    general cleaning
        different finishes 69
        methods and products
          69, 71
    pickup heights 93–95

re-stringing
    an acoustic guitar 83
    Bass E string 76–78
    case study 83–88
    D string 80
    G, B and E string 80–81
    machine heads 81
    pitching 83
    stretching the strings 89–91
    A string 78–80
    string gauges and changes 75–76
    string trees 88

Nashville Tune O Matic bridge 32
neck relief
    alternative applications 25–27
    measuring methods 19–20
    natural changes in 20
    setup and feel 22–23
    and truss rod adjustment 17–19, 25

re-fretting 149–151
    fret wire 154–156
    installation and finish 156–157
    preparation 151–152
    removing the frets 152–154
    tools 151

semi-hollow-bodied guitars 65–67
setup points
    assessment and adjustment 13–14
    maintenance 15
    neck relief adjustment 12
    starting and end goal 15
single-action truss rod 18
string height action
    alternatives 30–32
    fixed bridges 32–33
    individual-saddled bridges 33–34
    measurement 29–30
    micro-tilt adjustment 35
    order of assessment and
        adjustment 29
    pitch of the neck using shim 34–35
style and genre 11–12

TonePros bridge 33
tremolo system 43–44
truss rod 17
    access and adjustment 20–22
    types of 18

understand the numbers 11, 15

WD contact cleaner 67

First published in 2024 by
The Crowood Press Ltd
Ramsbury, Marlborough
Wiltshire SN8 2HR

enquiries@crowood.com

www.crowood.com

British Library Cataloguing-in-Publication Data
A catalogue record for this book is available from the British Library.

ISBN 978 0 7198 4363 1

Typeset by Simon and Sons
Cover design by Design Deluxe
Printed and bound in India by Parksons Graphics

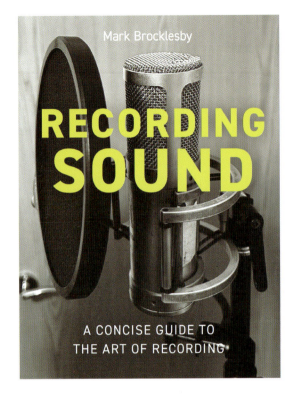

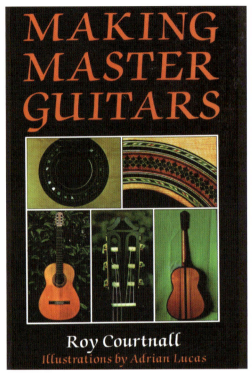

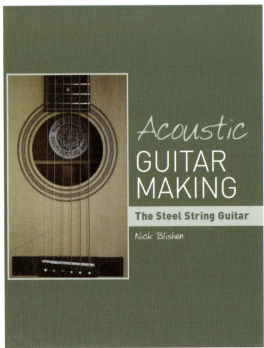

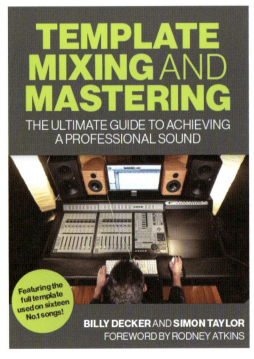